PRAISE FOR

Paul Angone offers a new voice to twentysomethings every-where, writing honestly about one of life's biggest transitions. At turns, *All Groan Up* is hilarious, poignant, and insightful. Angone relentlessly explores who God wants us to be rather than what God wants us to do — words everyone needs to hear, whatever their stage of life.

John Ortberg, author of *The Me I Want to Be*

Powerful, honest, heartfelt, and hilarious, this book is a must-read for anyone struggling to feel at home in their "groan-up" pants. If you're a twentysomething, or if you want to help a twen-tysomething, you need this book.

Megan Alexander, TV correspondent, *Inside Edition*

Relatable, funny, and inspiring, *All Groan Up* is an uplifting story about the redemption of hope when things don't go as planned. This book is must-read for anyone asking "What's next?"

Mike Foster, cofounder and chief chance officer of People of the Second Chance

This is it — the book every young person should read and every teacher and parent should have on hand. I don't think you can call yourself a grown-up without first reading this book.

Jeff Goins, author of *The Art of Work*

My twenties were like the new puberty — awkward, sweaty, weird, and life-changing, except no one warned me about them. Paul Angone's voice in *All Groan Up* is not just a warning. It is a conversation, a pep talk, wisdom mixed in with funny stories, and encouragement that not only can you survive this groan-up life; you can live it well.

Amena Brown, spoken word poet and author of
Breaking Old Rhythms

Paul Angone must live inside my house regularly filled with twentysomethings. He gets this generation like few people I know. This book is hilarious, insightful, brilliantly written, and filled with wisdom. Don't miss the opportunity to give this book to any young adult you know. They will read it because it's practical, and when they finish it, they will call it enjoyable, insightful, challenging, and even life-changing.

Jim Burns, PhD, president of HomeWord and author
of *Confident Parenting and Teenology: The Art of Raising Great Teenagers*

Our parents told us when we were children that we could do anything we set our minds to do. Our pastors said that God had a great plan for our lives. But after college, many of us got a sinking feeling that our parents were wrong, and we suspected our pastors were too. *All Groan Up* is a funny, hopeful, honest autobiography of a generation of people who feel their lives have too much potential and not enough purpose.

Matt Appling, author of *Life after Art*

The gigantic question, "Why am I here?" is written on everyone's heart. Fortunately for twentysomethings, this book will help answer the question and push them forward on a path of significance that will change their lives and the world around them.

Ken Coleman, author of *One Question* and host of
The Dave Ramsey Show Video Channel

Had me laughing out loud more times than I can count, sometimes literally to the point of tears! Paul Angone writes with a profundity and hilarity that feels like a nascent cross between Donald Miller and Bill Bryson. That's a high compliment. I think his words will be prophetic to a generation that is drowning in *potential.*

Mike Yankoski, author of *Under the Overpass*

Clever, insightful, and devilishly handsome, Paul Angone offers a book reminiscent of sharing a pint with an old friend. *All Groan Up* captures the confusion of early adulthood in a beautiful blend of candor and humor. This is a must-read for anyone wondering, *Okay, what now?*

Jamie Wright, theveryworstmissionary.com

Dr. Seuss's *Oh, the Places You'll Go!* may be the top gift at graduation, but this one should take its place. Writing with bravery and honesty, Paul Angone invites us behind his own search for purpose in a complicated world and shows us that the process is far more important than the destination. If you're at a crossroads in your own journey, you'll find his guide a welcome companion.

Wayne Jacobsen, author of *He Loves Me: Learning to Live in the Father's Affection*

For anyone wrestling with the provocative questions of "Who am I?" and "What am I going to do with who I am?" *All Groan Up* is a must-read. I encourage you to join Paul in his discovery of one of life's best-kept secrets, namely, that you can choose your future.

Raymond Rood, CEO, The Genysys Group

All Groan Up is part memoir, part real-time exploration, and part comforting coffee shop conversation with your best friend, who just happens to be a charming Italian author who has graciously offered his own missteps to help you avoid your own. Paul Angone brilliantly and honestly shares his relatable, heartbreaking, hilarious account of transitioning from frustrated graduate to faith-embracing adult. If you're in your twenties and questioning ANYTHING, this book is for you. Paul asks the big questions and isn't afraid to reveal his own worst fears, confessions, and lessons learned along the way. This book will lift you up when you're down and show you that no matter how many times you fall (face-first on a gravel sidewalk), you can and will get back up.

Jenny Blake, author of *Life after College*

All Groan Up in my humble opinion has the potential to be a bestseller. Paul Angone's blend of wit and wisdom is remarkable. He shares the lessons he has learned along life's way with such refreshing candor and insight that he should certainly help others on this journey of life.

David C. Bicker, PhD, professor emeritus and founding chair of the Department of Communication Studies at Azusa Pacific University

All Groan Up

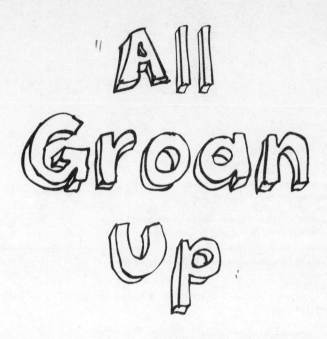

"All Groan Up

SEARCHING FOR SELF, FAITH, AND A FREAKING JOB!

PAUL ANGONE

ZONDERVAN®

ZONDERVAN

All Groan Up
Copyright © 2014 by Paul Angone

This title is also available as a Zondervan ebook.
Visit www.zondervan.com/ebooks.

Requests for information should be addressed to:
Zondervan, 3900 Sparks Dr. SE, Grand Rapids, Michigan 49546

Library of Congress Cataloging-in-Publication Data

Angone, Paul.
    All groan up : searching for self, faith, and a freaking job! / Paul Angone.-
1st [edition].
      pages cm
    ISBN 978-0-310-34135-2 (softcover)
    1. Young adults-Religious life. 2. Christian life. I. Title.
BV4529.2.A54 2015
248.8'4-dc23   2014041851

*Interior illustrations: Nathan Scheck (chapters zero, three, four, six, eight, ten,
eleven, twelve, thirteen, fourteen); Eddie Garcia (chapters one, two, five, seven,
nine, fifteen, sixteen)*
Interior design: Beth Shagene

First printing February 2015 / Printed in the United States of America

To my wife, Naomi —
for making me, and this book, much better.
To all the friends and family
whose encouragement and conversations
helped write these pages.

CONTENTS

Life transitions are like trying to ride a bull at a rodeo.
Everyone's watching.
You're so scared you slightly pee yourself.
If you can hold on for just eight seconds,
it's considered an outstanding accomplishment.
And when you fall, it's going to hurt like hell.

NOTE FROM
THE AUTHOR

Thank you for buying, acquiring, and/or borrowing this book!

And now, I ask you to stop reading it.

Yes, stop, and then consider reading this book alongside a group of friends.

First, so more people buy it — *enter cash register noise here for audiobook* — and second, so you're not trying to do this groan-up life alone. We need community.

This book is the most vulnerable story I could tell, and I hope it becomes a safe place for you to wrestle with hard questions and find some answers. But before you do, look around at the friends right next to you who are struggling to climb. We all could use a cup of coffee and a good conversation. How about asking them to join you on this journey?

I went into college graduation believing I was now trained and equipped to go change the world.

And if not to change the world, at least to make a serious difference.

And if not to make a serious difference, at least to make some serious money.

And if not any money, at least be working a job that I enjoyed.

And if a job I didn't really enjoy, at least a job that sounded *enjoyable* — something I could spin to my friends as I convinced them of my amazing life. Even if it wasn't really.

With college diploma in hand, I was ready to be used by God and man in big ways. A college diploma meant answers. A college diploma meant doors flung open, where everything is up for grabs.

So why now, years later, do my hands still feel like they're in pockets full of Super Glue?

To make matters worse, I have other friends whose hands are glueless. They started grabbing success the minute they stepped into the real world.

One of those friends (I call them friends, but secretly I loathe them just a little now) is Mike Yankoski, who purposely became homeless for five months, then wrote a life-changing and powerful book about it called *Under the Overpass.* Now he's traveling everywhere speaking about this experience. Such vision, such strength, such hope, such excitement, such purpose. Thanks,

Mike. While you're at it, can you come over and kick my little dog, BeauJo, who has to wear diapers because he can't control his bladder?

Another one of my friends, Brent, recently came back from El Salvador, where he helped start and sustain eight different businesses for the local economy. Right after he returned, he received a random call asking if he wanted to jump on a private jet and fly with influential guys like Rick Warren (author of *The Purpose Driven Life*) to Uganda to help with peace efforts and business development.

Brent told me one amazing story after another about his spur-of-the-moment trip to Africa and Switzerland (I forgot to mention this added jaunt to Switzerland). During one of their flights, Brent explained, he glanced at the computer screen of the gentleman sitting next to him, only to see him working on a speech for (then current) President Bush, which good old George W. would be giving the following Tuesday. My friend sat next to, conversed with, and bounced ideas off one of the U.S. president's inner circle whilst — *pause for effect* — flying to Switzerland in a private jet!

I remember the night Brent dropped in unexpectedly and told me about his trip. It was a cool, crisp evening. I was sitting on a brown, furry beanbag called the Lovesack that was purchased at a yard sale. As Brent told his story, a very large part of me was very excited for him as I sat on the edge of my Lovesack in awe and anticipation. A very large part of me felt very proud of my friend. A large and overwhelming part.

But then there was this small, little voice that kept popping up like an angry squirrel that believes he owns your bird feeder. Sure it was small, but it made its presence known. *Paul*, the voice asked, *what are you doing right now?*

"Well, I'm still trying to find my way. I'm doing — "

No, no, the small voice said with a chuckle. *Not what are you doing* in life, *but literally* right at this moment — *what are you doing?*

Then the joke hit me. Here my friend Brent is explaining how he's trying to change the world in a dramatic way. Flying to Africa, chatting it up with world leaders. And what was I doing while he's telling me all this? Eating a piece of chicken (all right, not actual chicken but chicken-flavored Top Ramen) while icing my hamstring, which I had torn during a slow-pitch softball game.

Slow-pitch softball! The "sport" that fifty-five-year-old men with a gut the size of Fort Worth, swinging a bat with beers in both hands, can excel at.

At the very least I could've been icing my hamstring that I'd hurt sprinting into a burning building to save a three-year-old with terminal cancer.

As Brent told his hilarious story of the plane not being able to find runway space in Zurich, I flashed back years ago to my Smug College Self, that arrogant kid who was untouchable. Thriving there in that peaceful, safe collegiate womb. Smiling, dreaming, thinking big — knowing that once I was really born, my life would be made into a movie someday. And if not a movie, at least a TV miniseries.

How I wished I could've gone back and just slapped that know-it-all grin off his face. I would've loved to tell him the truth — that someday he would be on a giant, hairy beanbag, broke and unemployed, eating his last Top Ramen while his friends did all the big things he'd always dreamed of. But there, back in the womb, would I have even listened?

CHAPTER ONE

It was so cozy. The best La-Z-Boy on the market. Complete tranquility never to be duplicated. Our only responsibility was to set our seats to "relax." Comfort only embryonic fluid could offer.

And for nine straight months, relax we did. How could we not? Lights dimmed to a perfect sleeping level. Never too hot, never too cold. Soundproof walls impervious to dogs barking, blenders mixing, people yelling.

And the food. Oh, the food! Delicious and delivered directly to our stomachs. None of this opening cans or reheating leftovers for us. No sir, it was seven-course cuisine in a tube.

And the best part? The only person you had to deal with was you. And not you as you are today, but a you with no wrongs.

You hadn't yet stolen any cookies from the pantry. Hadn't tried to look up the dress of your fourth-grade teacher. Hadn't called your best friend stupid or told your parents you hate them. No failures, no history of disappointments, no shameful secrets, no insecurities as blaring as that zit on your nose you'd be blessed with come age fourteen.

Nope. Just ten fingers, ten toes, a couple appendages hanging off your side. Pretty simple. You had yourself pretty much figured out.

Life was sweet in the womb. A couple of posters over there, a plant or two thataway, maybe someday a flat-screen TV. You had big plans to stay there forever. It was comfort; it was safety; it was the best five-star hotel no money could buy.

To have faith that life would end up smelling like a twelve-dozen-rose bouquet was no stretch of the imagination. It wasn't much of a leap to trust that your cocoon would shield you from all harm. That was the standard, not the exception. Everything around you said so. Until one fateful day.

What the (insert expletive here)!

But the womb was a liar, a cheat, false advertising to the extreme — a fact that every human being learns a bit too late, as tranquility turns to *what the* … in about 5.7 seconds. Comfortably dimmed lights switch to a 250-watt medical spot lamp pointed directly in your eyes. La-Z-Boyesque embryonic cushions violently transition to huge hands yanking on your head, turning your neck a direction you never knew it could go.

"Whoa. Hey, *hey!* Son … of … a …!" Cutting, bleeding, screaming. And worst of all, when you finally make it through, you're naked. With a bunch of people staring at you. And you realize for the first time (and probably not the last) that naked you isn't all that attractive. Your body resembles less a Michelangelo and more that thing your cat found in the backyard and dragged into the middle of the family room.

Would it have killed somebody to give us a little heads-up? At least put up a couple of warning signs along the way out?

"Proceed with Caution."

"This Might Sting a Little."

"Severe Turbulence Ahead."

"Swim Back Upstream! Swim for Your Life!"

"This Gets a Whole Lot Worse before It Gets Better."

A Few Years Later

Birth is our introduction to transition. What a word that is — *transition*. It rolls off the tongue so sophisticatedly, so refined. Like an English gentleman sending his regrets.

But that's not really how *transition* should sound. Not when it brings glaring lights and screams and 180-degree neck twists.

I retell our dramatic entry into the world because I experienced another birth-like transition. In one terrifying motion, this transition ripped my comfortable little life from its slumber, leaving me crying and naked again.

So what happened on this terrifying day?

Well, this is where more esteemed authors would describe the car crash that put them in the hospital for fifteen months, or the day they learned they had cancer. And the rest of their book would unfold an uplifting story of courage and triumph.

Well, that's not me. Nope, not a speck of cancer. And my beautiful Honda Civic hatchback that I started driving during my senior year of high school is running as smoothly as ever.

No, my own life-altering transition is something commonly understood to be a cause for celebration.

It was a day that I prayed time and time again would finally come.

It was a day my parents and I spent thousands upon thousands upon thousands of dollars for. It was a day extended parts of my family came out to cheer, sporting blue and green plastic fold-up chairs and yelling embarrassing things at inopportune times.

This day, this event, this supposed rocket-launch-into-the-rest-of-my-life: college graduation!

I crossed that stage on a sunny day in May, shook a few hands, flashed my "got everything figured out" grin, and before I could even wrap my fingers around that diploma, someone was grabbing my head, ripping me out. In an instant, I was a *gradu-what the heck do I do now?*

Who Wants Cake?

During my graduation party, I couldn't move. The smiling faces, the excited handshakes, the sentiments of joy and congratulations. Aunts and uncles pinching me on the cheeks like they did two decades before.

Everything whipped around me so fast I couldn't move. I felt like the deer stuck on the highway, exposed and vulnerable in the oncoming semi's headlights of "So, Paul, what are your plans for the *future*?"

The future? Heck if I knew. Guests tossed prying questions in my face like live hand grenades.

I'd just been born, for graduation's sake! My goal right now is to successfully balance this corner piece of cake the size of a Barcalounger on this sturdy coaster-of-a-plate, made from wet, used newspapers, while looking around my house that seven guys have been living in all year and desperately trying to see a way we could ever successfully clean this place so they'll actually let us leave. Once I get all that straightened out, then maybe I'll be able to block your graciously lobbed grenades with my ten-part prospectus for the years ahead.

Complications

Everything we thought we knew about ourselves and God and our role in this crazy two-sheets-to-the-wind world changed the day we actually entered it — whether our cocoon exit came on that first day out of school or on the job or in marriage. Whatever the situation, we've all had that *"Oh, crap, so this is what real life is"* kind of moment. When everything we were so sure about quickly becomes obsolete.

Sun in our eyes. Rash on our legs. Poop that used to just float away, now stuck in the most uncomfortable places imaginable. All we can do is cry. And cry we do.

The womb apparently was not the accurate teacher of reality like we once thought. On that first day out, the hard, cold learning began for us all.

But with it came some perks of living outside our former insulation as well. Taking that first step, eating that first chocolate chip cookie, sliding down our first waterslide, petting our first dog, getting that tingly feeling the first time we really noticed that special *someone*.

So that later, if you asked us to go back into the womb, we would decline. That would be gross. Sure, life immersed in the outside can sting. A lot. But life in the womb wasn't much of a life after all. To actually live, we had to be born.

Let Life Begin

At least that's what I keep telling myself. Because I'm realizing that living on the outside is harder than I thought. And some simple, straightforward words are much more complicated now: *faith, hope, purpose, passion, paying bills, lumbar support, budgeting,* et cetera. I actually have to know something about these words now. The *future* was going to be on a test to be named later, and somehow *later* had just snuck up on me and smacked me with the edge of that $300 textbook I refused to sell back for $6.33.

In my cocoon, lying there in gooey goodness, I grew all kinds of faith. I didn't doubt for a second I was safe. In babyese I would cry out, "Here I am, Lord. Send me!" I envisioned my words leaving the womb and traveling across the vastness of creation, over the horizon, to where God sat waiting and listening to my cry, waiting to respond.

But now that I'm out, I hear no answer. Only the echo of my cry in return. Is the problem my hearing or his voice?

So now what? Is it up to God or up to me? If it's up to God, what's he doing about it? If it's up to me ... where do I even start?

As I'm carried out of the hospital and introduced to sights my eyes have never seen, I'm exhilarated ... and terrified. The fear and excitement of a world of unknowns keep me whispering, "Got to be born to really live; got to be born to really live." Fingers crossed. *Got to be born to really live.*

CHAPTER TWO

TOP RAMEN DREAMER

Six months after college is a magical time for a college graduate as your friends — Stafford, Perkins, and the nice man at the bank — decide to retract their hand of grace.

Wait, I actually have to pay these loans back? I thought college loans were like Monopoly money. Someday, in a land far, far away, I'd hand over a couple of pink fives and a few blue fifties, and we'd call it even.

That or someone would slip me a "get out of jail free" card, like Bono announcing a year of loan forgiveness, *on him*, for all of us middle-class suckers whose parents somehow made enough money to not receive any financial aid, yet somehow concurrently didn't make enough money to even pay for half of first-year English.

So wait, Ms. Sallie Mae — I have to pay *how* much, for *how* long? Who knew you owned Boardwalk with a hotel and I'd apparently been a resident there these last four years? So I won't Pass Go for two decades. No big deal.

Who has money for loans anyway? Rent is my more pressing reality. Also, for some reason, it takes food to live. And people charge money for it. What's up with that?

Then there are little things like car insurance, health insurance, and the miscellaneous fun excursions to the mechanic for a blown head gasket on my aforementioned Honda Civic.

"Changing the world" has quickly jumped into the backseat

and is taking a nap, while the "reality of continued living" is taking over.

What makes it worse is that I'm still around chipper, know-it-all college students who keep asking, "Hey, Paul, what are *you* doing with your life?" With their little rosy cheeks and that quiver of excitement in their voice that *knows* they will make their first million within a year after graduation.

Another thing my professors forgot to teach me was how to lovingly reply, "Working at Starbucks," without wanting to pull out a flask of vodka, take a swig, and then pour just a dash on their clothes and light it on fire.

Not to burn them severely, of course, but just to put the fear of God in them a little, so they know never again to ask me how "life" is. And, of course, to give me a little chuckle as I watch them stop, drop, and roll.

Silly college kids.

But just a class ago, I was one of them — eager to start my future, completely assured the red carpet would precede all my steps. I remember secretly wondering what was wrong with all those twentysomethings who were waiting tables or working boring cubicle jobs. *Come on, how hard could it be?*

I thought the only problem after college would be picking *which* amazing job offer to take, like five popular girls all asking me to go to prom. Unfortunately, just like in high school, they somehow all lost my number.

So all those premed students — the ones I mocked in school as they scurried to their labs on Friday nights — were now smiling from ear to ear as they stepped into top medical schools like Columbia, Stanford, and UCLA while I enthusiastically stepped into my local temp agency.

My Own Worst Enemy

Temp agencies are a world I would not want my worst enemies subjected to. Mainly because I envision my worst enemies working deep in the coal mines of Siberia guarded by Arctic wolves, so I figure I'd give them a pass on the whole temp agency process to land such a job. I know, full of grace I am.

If you ever feel you need a good humbling experience, spend four years of your life mastering the liberal arts, then take the incredibly challenging aptitude test at your local temp agency:

Question 1: If you have a file that begins with a Q, what drawer would you put it in?

> a. A – E
> b. F – K
> c. L – O
> d. P – T
> e. U – Z

I answered *c.* Purely out of spite.

My roommate, Rob, went to the same temp agency, and they placed him at a warehouse packaging nutcrackers. Big wooden Christmas nutcrackers. By himself, packing one nutcracker after another. Him and his degree in computer science keeping him company.

When Rob had seen enough nutcrackers, they placed him at a "Boob Factory" (or so we called it). It was a silicone plant where he did computer entry work. He worked there for a year. Three hundred sixty-five days gone so that women could go from a 34B to a 34D.

And when I told the temp agency I didn't want to specialize in nuts or boobs, they set me up with something even better.

I had an interview to become (*drumroll, please*) a used-airplane-parts sales assistant. Dream job, here I come!

Interview Time

Now this was my first real out-of-college interview so, understandably, I was nervous as I walked into the office. Not about messing up the interview, mind you, which is probably what a person should be worried about at their first interview. No, I was scared because I'd just realized I must have been flying around this whole time in airplanes with *used parts*.

I don't know about you, but I want the wings that are carrying my rear end thirty thousand feet above the ground to be brand-spanking-new.

But with $67 in my checking/savings account (they were one and the same), I put those concerns aside and prayed they would just give me the chance to be the best little used-airplane-parts sales assistant this side of the Mississippi.

I spent four hours interviewing with the entire office. Shaking one hand after another, smiling with feigned excitement at the possibility of fulfilling my *childhood dream* of being a used-airplane-parts sales assistant person.

But in interview number four, I became aware of some strange similarities within this office.

First, no one ever smiled. Each interviewer's slow, monotonous voice describing the *exciting opportunities* that came with my position seemed noticeably contradictory. (Thank you, deduction skills via aforementioned liberal arts degree.)

Second, each interviewer used the exact same sentences when describing the "wonder" that was the company, the "love" they had for working there, and the "absolute thrill" of used airplane parts.

Soon I was completely convinced — not about my future working there, but about the fact that all of them were either:

a. terrorist alien drones sent to earth to sabotage our airline industry

b. prisoners who had disrespected the Used-Airplane-Parts Feudal Lord of Santa Barbara and were being held captive

c. regular people who desperately wanted to escape but were being sedated with gas through the overhead vents

d. regular people who had become comfortable living crappily ever after

The final interviewer wasn't much older than me — she was cute with long legs and hair that told me it wished it was outside. As she recited the Feudal Alien Lord's mandatory brainwashed spiel, I wanted to lean over and whisper, "Let's get out of here."

Whether she was alien or human, it seemed inhumane to leave her caged up here.

We could bust out of this place together, jump in my Honda Civic hatchback, and fly down the highway at seventy-five miles per hour to Mexico (after seventy-five miles per hour, everything in my car begins to shake and things get a little dicey). Me and my used-airplane-parts refugee could start our new lives together, selling deep-sea fishing trips and books about her true account of survival and rescue from the Lord of Used Airplane Parts.

But I knew she wouldn't come. She was here. She wasn't going anywhere. And I desperately wanted to leave.

As I walked toward the front door as the hiring manager said they'd be in touch, I began staring closely at the vents above, wondering how management pulled off pumping in so much poisonous air. Because it was either that, or everyone was, in fact, *this* miserable.

For their sakes, I prayed they were being gassed.

Here's Your Life

Two days later, the chipper lady at the temp agency called and told me the job was mine. Excitedly she started going over the paperwork, telling me they wanted me to start the next week.

As she rambled on, a strange thing began to happen. I felt a sickening sensation rising from my stomach into my chest, like the time I ate a spoonful of chunky milk thinking it was cottage cheese.

Was I really going to do this? Did I really get a college education to be the guy with a pulse who could handle this *challenging* and *rewarding* job? Was I going to devote the next six months, year, three years, my life, to used airplane parts? Was I willingly going to become their prisoner?

"I need some time to think about this," I quickly interrupted her.

"Excuse me. What was that? It's yours. You start next Monday. So come in first thing tomorrow, and we'll — "

"No, I need to think about whether I want to take the job."

"What?"

"I just don't know if I see myself as a used-airplane-parts sales assistant person."

"Paul, it's a great opportunity with a lot of *upward mobility*." A catchall phrase to make a bottom-dweller job seem worthwhile.

"Um, I just don't think I can," I squeaked out, not knowing if I was trying to convince her or myself.

"Well, Paul, they absolutely loved you and want you to start right away. So just come to my office — "

"No ... no, I don't think I can," I said it again as my confidence and resolve grew. "Actually, I know I can't. I'm sorry, but you're just going to have to tell them thanks but no thanks."

We both sat in silence for about ten seconds. Little grunts and sharp spurts of breaths pierced through the receiver like little audio daggers. I could feel my chipper little helper losing her chipperness.

"I went to a lot of trouble finding you this interview."

"I know you did, and I'm very thankful for all your help."

More silence. Then my friendly little elf at the temp agency did a wonderful impression of Darth Vader, with just a dash of Satan.

"Listen here, you can't come to a temp agency, get offered a job, and then turn it down. That's not how it works. You're going to take this job."

"No I'm not!"

Click.

Apparently, Darth Satan decided our conversation was over.

Prime Rib

So I turned down my one job offer. Sure, I was barely scraping by, living on a steady diet of year-old Top Ramen and water. But I would rather be a Top Ramen Dreamer than a Prime Rib Realist.

My dad, on the other hand, did not share that sentiment. When I told him I turned down the job, he didn't applaud my resolve. He didn't pat me on the back. He didn't chuckle at my witty little Top Ramen Dreamer, Prime Rib Realist analogy. He only sat there and listened. Then he said one thing, with the frankness that dads get paid the big bucks for: "But son, it was a job."

Thank you, Dad. I'm aware it was a job. It was a "work there and become an alcoholic in three months" job.

I don't want to sell airplane parts. I don't want to pack nut-crackers like my roommate Rob. And while we're on the topic, I also don't want to be a doctor. I don't want to be a lawyer. Or a teacher, farmer, pastor, actor, missionary, et cetera, et cetera. I've become quite good at pinpointing what I don't want. But what I *do* want — now that's another question.

There's the rub. There's the fact that drives me crazy. I feel like my job search after graduation was like riding in a helicopter over Rocky Mountain National Park, with the pilot telling me my dream job was down there in those trees somewhere, right before he shoved me out the door.

The fall was exhilarating, until I smacked the ground.

CHAPTER THREE

BEST YEARS OF YOUR LIFE

think dads are paid on commission for saying certain phrases. Probably around ten cents every time they utter, "Money doesn't grow on trees," or "Were you raised in a barn?"

My dad definitely had his fair share of go-to clichés, which I always listened to. Really, I didn't have any other choice.

One, my dad was a pastor of a church, so he was hearing directly from God on at least a weekly basis. Second, he looked like the Italian mobsters' secondhand man who rose to the top for his love of hearing bones crack. And I was pretty sure the pastor thing was an elaborate ruse to hide his real "import, export" business. So disagreeing with my dad, by any account, never seemed like a wise idea.

Above all phrases, my dad has uttered one particular platitude more times than I can count. Whenever I complained or times seemed hard or life seemed boring, I could always count on his response: "Enjoy it, son; these are the best days of your life."

Like the old pair of slippers he pulled from the guy who couldn't pay his loan, it was his phrase that he kept slipping on, no matter how bad it smelled.

Really? The Best?

I'm always amazed how, in good conscience and with a straight face, he can seriously rattle off this statement time and time again and mean it every time. Common sense tells me it can't always be true.

Elementary school: "Three recesses a day, no homework, Beanie Weenies in your lunch box, no complexities, no hassles. Enjoy it, Paul. These are the best years of your life."

Middle school: "Playing as many sports as you can, shaving for the first time, little to no homework. Make the most of it, Paul; it only gets harder. This is the best time in your life."

High school: "I know these football two-a-days in the heat don't seem fun right now. But the camaraderie! The sweat! The blood! Oh, man, I get goose bumps just talking about it. Soak it up, Paul — they're the best days of your life."

College: "Getting pizza at 2:00 a.m. Water-ballooning your professors. These are absolutely the best..."

Best years of your life. What a sham of a phrase. Only when they take a vote from everyone who's died and then come to a consensus, will I listen.

"What's that, Socrates? You suggest the early thirties are the best years? And you, Augustine? You're saying early teens? All right, everyone; let's vote."

Actually, as I look back, despite the neurotic and illogical way my dad kept using the phrase, I kept believing it. Never while I was actually living and breathing in that particular "best" season. No. I only believed it a couple of days before it ended, and then for a year or so afterward. Once the season was over and gone and I couldn't go back — that's when I knew it must have been the best.

Spin the Big Wheel

Take what was happening for me in middle school, for example. Eighth grade was my Acne Grand Opening, with a zit on the tip of my nose the circumference of Cuba. It was so big that rumors spread it was actually a tumor. Which, of course, I didn't deny. Because you can make fun of the kid with a pimple but not the kid with a tumor. So I let that cancer rumor run as long as it had legs.

Then there was that fun little battle at the back of my throat. A voice that hadn't quite figured out what to be. Some days it sounded female, some days male, some days a little mixture of both. Like going through a daily sex change. Sometimes I'd go to the bathroom just to make sure everything was still there.

Puberty is the teenager's Russian roulette. We could go overnight from popular to a gangly mess. Girls and guys all had to spin the Big Wheel to see what horribly awkward thing we might get to live with for the next three years.

"Come on, thick mustache with hair nowhere else."

"Come on, teeth coming in sideways through my cheeks."

"Come on, legs that grow five times faster than the rest of my body."

"Come on, boobs that don't grow at all, giving me the nickname Bee Stings till I'm twenty-five years old."

Middle school. If God came down right now and told me he'd give the world complete peace for a thousand years if I'd just relive middle school, I would politely answer, "Thanks but no thanks. I'll take my chances with war."

I didn't like middle school then and wouldn't want to relive it now. But here's the funny thing: At one point in my life I completely convinced myself that middle school had, in fact, been my best years.

It started at the end of eighth grade, when everyone came together in a fit of nostalgia. Just weeks earlier it was, "I hate middle school because of this and that." But the day before graduation, it was, "Oh, man, I don't know how I'll live without this and that."

A couple of weeks earlier, we were lighting a bag of poop on fire and putting it on Mrs. Franklin's front porch; now we're waiting in line for Mrs. Franklin to sign our yearbook.

It's funny how being freaked out about the future makes you really appreciate the past.

In those middle school days, loyalties among friends lasted only as long as that zit on my nose. Yet when middle school was over, we cried as we sang, "Friends are friends forever ..."

Infamous Back Acne

Then came those first excruciating months of high school. In the midst of that anguish, our selective memory process completely took over. Middle school really had been heaven. Now we called Mrs. Franklin every night and three times on weekends just to hear again her sweet, angelic voice.

As a freshman I still had all the awkward characteristics I dreaded in middle school, but now I had two thousand people to make fun of me for them.

I tried to sneak through the incredibly packed halls, going unnoticed with the knockoff shoes my mom bought for me at Payless. But with my every step, a man with a megaphone followed behind, yelling, "Hey, everyone! Don't be fooled — these shoes are not cool. And he has acne! Crowd around and laugh, everybody! Yes, feel free to point!"

Even worse was the fact that my acne spread like a tropical disease, not only throughout my face, but to my back and chest as well.

Thanks, Puberty Fairy. I like your sister who specializes in teeth much better.

At least since I had no plans to be the freshman who went traipsing through the halls topless, my back acne would not be a problem. Then I saw my first class schedule:

English: 7:45 – 8:45 a.m. — Room B104
Algebra: 8:55 – 9:55 a.m. — Room D303
U.S. History: 10:05 – 11:05 a.m. — Room Good-Luck-Finding-It
Biology: 12:00 – 1:00 p.m. — Room A101
Swimming: 1:15 – Eternity — The Pool — *Enjoy!*

Swimming! No, no, *no.* This can't be. It must be some sort of typographic error or sick joke.

Mandatory swimming class for all freshmen — now there was a bright idea from the principal. Get three hundred of the most awkward-looking, self-conscious, horribly terrified people and make them take off their clothes in front of each other and jump into a freezing pool with enough chlorine to kill a small elephant. Every Monday, Wednesday, Friday.

My back acne was going to be famous.

Sophomore year didn't get much better. In football, I was placed on the dreaded Scout Team. This meant that in practice we had to go against the starting varsity offense so they could perfect their plays on a slower, weaker bunch. It was like Darwin rose from the grave and wanted to prove his theories on awkward teenagers. We were like a mixed bunch of turtles, chipmunks, and rogue ostriches taking on a team of steroid-infused rhinos.

I won the Scout Team Award that year, which I think meant I excelled at being flattened on my back better than anyone else.

Junior year got better, though high school was still a steep, rocky climb. Literally every day you could throw away three years of image management by falling down the stairs during a passing period or throwing up in the trash can in the middle of class. That one reputation-shattering event, which forever became a nickname.

But before I knew it, I was a senior, and high school was actually enjoyable. I had some good friends, and now I was the one knocking the sophomore Scout Team guys on their backs. For the first time, middle school was remembered for what it really was — both good and bad. Mrs. Franklin retired, and I didn't even bother to go to the party. High school was now the best time ever. I went to parties, skipped classes, matured, learned. And *bam*, it was over.

Spoiled Paradise

Then college rolled around. This step was bigger; therefore, so was the fear.

The riskier the jump, the more ambulances waiting on the side.

Maybe you picked a college like I did. One of your friend's second cousin's uncle said he knew someone who went to this great school and loved it. Plus, the girl on the front of the brochure looked pretty cute. So you go there. Even though it's in the middle of Nebraska.

Then the process happened all over again. Nostalgia, anxiety, loneliness. I soon realized the cute girl on the brochure was one of the five attractive girls in all of Nebraska. Different colleges just hired her to be on their promotional pieces. (Just kidding. I wish they all could be Nebraska girls.) For a year I stuck it out in always windy, too-hot-too-cold Nebraska.

Then I heard about this college in California. So although

I loved Nebraska as much as an eye infection, I thought I just might find life a tad more enjoyable in Santa Barbara, California.

But even in Santa Barbara, the process began once more. It was hard transferring into a school as a sophomore. Everyone else had their shared freshman experience, and their friendships were pretty set. So yes, I was lonely. A little depressed. I asked God why and wondered if he really knew what was best.

Eventually I made a friend. Then another. I had an amazing class, then one more. The scales slowly fell from my eyes and the fog lifted, and I realized I was truly in paradise.

My senior year, I lived with six of my closest friends in a house with a hot tub on a deck that perfectly overlooked the Pacific Ocean. The yard was filled with avocado, lemon, and orange trees. I scheduled all my classes on Tuesday and Thursday so I always had a four-day weekend, with a Wednesday in between to catch my breath.

Spoiled paradise, utterly and completely.

Seeing a Pattern?

With every transition I've faced, I've struggled to find meaning in my new existence. I've sworn that God, this time, had finally forsaken me. This time he was off saving some kid in Romania and just flat-out forgot about me.

But I've always made it. Sure, I've been lonely and depressed. I've had zits, chemistry finals, relationships ending in heartbreak. I've had the good, the bad, the mediocre. In every transition. But I can look back and see that it always led to something better somehow.

I mean, what if with every scary transition I actually had my way and refused to move forward? I'd now be walking around with that little elementary desk stuck to my butt. And who wants that?

The Best?

So if things progress as they always have, I'll look back some-day at this postgraduation season and call it "the best years of my life." The time when I had everything up for grabs. The time when I could be whatever I wanted. The time before a mortgage and three kids.

But Dad never told me, "Get ready, son; those early adult years are the best days. The entry-level job, fifty-dollar savings account, never-ending questions, and trying to be an adult when actual *adults* know you're just playing dress-up. Yes, those were the absolute best."

Adulthood. When you're no longer able to chalk up mistakes and failures as simply part of childhood adolescence, a part of learning and growing. When the process is over and the grace to mess up is packed away with the baseball cards and Barbie dolls.

When you start back at the bottom like you're in first grade all over again, except all your classmates are in their mid-forties with 401(k)s and back problems they somehow blame on you.

No, Dad never said the process of transitioning from *growing* to *grown* was the best. He fell strangely silent at my graduation party. He just shook my hand and gave me a slight smirk.

I should've known something was the matter.

The Present

So now I sit as someone's employee, fondly remembering my most recent best years ever.

Let the cycle continue.

Because life after college is *work*. And not the summer-job "work" where you flirt with members of the opposite sex, joke with friends, and in two and a half months you're done. No, this work lasts twelve months a year. And when you're done with that ...

"Johnny, tell them what they've won!"

"Well, Alex, they've won *twelve more months* of monotonous, mind-numbing work!"

No week off for Thanksgiving, month off for Christmas, week off for spring break, just to somehow make it to your three-months-off summer.

Life became a perfectly designed rut. Life became a twelve-months-a-year struggle. Life became a chore, worse than cleaning the toilet after your little brother had the stomach flu.

Life became, *God help me*, a cubicle.

CHAPTER FOUR

When my friend Stephanie compared her life to the classic children's picture book *Are You My Mother?* I identified with her right away. And told her on the spot I was going to steal the metaphor. So that's what I'm doing.

Remember the story? A little bird is hatched, only to quickly realize it's all alone. It goes around asking cows, dogs, anyone, "Are you my mother?"

That's how I feel.

"Excuse me? Are you my job? Are you my future? Are you my passion? Are you it? Are you my life? Come on, someone must know."

I'm supposed to be taking down my dream job like a hunter snagging a prize deer. Instead I'm asking the deer for directions on how to get back home.

Job Hunter

Should I really be surprised that the job hunt produces severe anxiety? It's a "hunt" for survival stakes — battling countless twentysomethings who are just as hungry as I am, with our future coming down to who will win this fight.

At college graduation they should've handed out spears and some sort of harpoon-like devices along with the diplomas. Twentysomethings looking for a job is like the *Hunger Games* without the cameras or any interaction with Jennifer Lawrence.

People say our generation is entitled. In some ways, maybe. But we're also fiercely competitive with an obsession for success. We don't know how to fail. And even when we do fail, we're pretty sure we actually won. The idiot keeping score must've had a crush on the winner.

We grew up in a competitive, bell-curve, wait-list society. Fighting for a spot on the team, in a school, at a job, for the win. We don't want blue ribbons because we feel entitled to them; we want them because we've been in a cage match to win them our entire lives. Now, the stakes for those blue ribbons are just slightly higher.

I feel like I'm ten years old again, hanging on that pull-up bar like a rock climber about to fall to his death — all with my entire third-grade class snickering behind me. I don't want to fail and end up again with the dreaded, patronizing puke-yellow ribbon of Honorable Mention. The non-award. Granting the lucky recipient that extra boost of self-confidence, like working at McDonald's and being runner-up to the employee of the month.

I will work as hard as I can for that blue ribbon, but what are the ground rules for how to win one? I have nothing against jobs or hard work; what I have a problem with is hard work in a field I don't really care about, to be promoted to a job I never wanted, in a cubicle that makes me ever so slightly die inside.

Cubicle Crazy

Is there more than this? I seem to ask that question over and over now that I'm out of college. As we begin the rest of our lives, is this really it? Is this what life is going to be about?

Do I want to live as someone's employee, accepting a paycheck (or sedative, whatever you want to call it) in exchange for my creativity, hard work, ideas, and life, which someone else profits from?

A couple of careers. A couple of kids. A couple of houses. A couple of cars. A couple of spouses (for some). A couple of last breaths. Then I'm done.

Sure, that's a little oversimplified, a little bleak. But you must understand that I'm covertly writing this right now at work, sitting in my office composed of shoulder-high gray cubicle walls.

Yes, I finally did garner gainful employment. After numerous interviews, my first "real" job wasn't as a used-airplane-parts pusher, but as an admissions counselor for my college alma mater. I couldn't come to grips with the fact that I'd actually graduated, so why not just be *that guy* who still eats in his college cafeteria?

I must reiterate here that I truly did love my time in college. I think the small school I went to (and then worked for) did many, many things right. It truly was the most amazing learning community I've ever been a part of.

The fact that I loved my school days so much makes my job selling the school easy, yet difficult. Easy because I get to travel to Texas, Colorado, Washington, Oregon, and California, telling story after story about my amazing classes, amazing friends, and amazing college life.

Difficult because then I go back to a room in some no-name hotel where I watch reruns of *Friends* while eating ~~two~~ three bags of M&Ms from the vending machine down the hall, sitting alone in my boxers on a bedspread that probably around 1,635 people have had sex on, which hasn't been cleaned since New Kids on the Block was cranking out hits.

That's my night.

Then the next day I'm back, selling high school kids on a glamorous future if they just follow in my footsteps. I wonder if they'd still be nodding and smiling excitedly during the day if they could see where those footsteps led me every night.

Or if they could behold my glamorous gray cubicle that awaited me back at home.

A cubicle, as defined by *Webster's*, is "a small partitioned space." *What in the world?* Who decided it was a good idea to make human beings spend a vast portion of their lives in "a small partitioned space"?

Humans are not intended to live encased within rainy-day gray walls. We're not rats. This is not a science experiment. These are our *lives* we're talking about here.

Is it too much to ask for walls that extend all the way to the ceiling? Call me crazy, but I thought that was the defining characteristic of a wall. A piece of padded material that extends only five feet from the ground seems less a wall and more a mistake.

I'm guessing some lazy construction worker in New Jersey probably birthed the idea of the cubicle. He ran out of building materials and finished every office five feet short, passing it off as the new "in" look.

Quick question: Do you think a cubicle wall is *flammable*? Just asking.

Living for Chocolate Frosting

I haven't always been so anti-cubicle and, therefore, anti-life. But each day encased in a cube is another day falling deeper into a pit I never wanted to crawl into.

When I realized that TV and movie satires about the inane

ridiculousness of work had switched from being comedies to very personal, deeply depressing documentaries, I took my first sick day. I stayed in bed, drank lots of water, and ate chicken noodle soup, hoping it had the ability to fight suffocating depression as well as the sniffles.

I liked watching TV shows that made fun of mindless cubicle life because they were ridiculously funny, not because they were ridiculously true. I used to laugh at the awkwardly dis-impassioned and overall meaningless lives of the characters like I laughed at the smelly kid in my seventh-grade English class. It was funny because it wasn't me.

Then one day you realize that people call you *Smelly Kid #2* or that the promise of chocolate frosting is all that gets you through the day — and it's a lot less hilarious.

I remember the exact moment I realized this. It happened in the back corner of my office with ten other employees as we sang the most depressing rendition of "Happy Birthday" I've ever heard. We sounded like POWs singing to a fellow prisoner as we cut up a piece of birthday cake right before our daily torture.

But the song wasn't the most depressing part. Not even close. Much more depressing was realizing how excited I was for a piece of cake. I was ecstatic. A piece of cake that would take my mind off my cubicle cage just for a moment. I didn't even know whose birthday it was, nor did I really care. All I knew was that there was chocolate frosting, and chocolate frosting had become my reason for showing up to work.

I thought the Freshman Fifteen was bad. It's nothing compared to the Cubicle Cincuenta. My waistline expanding as my big dreams deflate.

The Sanctity of Home

With cubicles not exactly kicking off my career with an enviable bang, most days I couldn't wait to get home. Like a kid rushing down the stairs to see if he could spot his new bike under the Christmas tree, at five o'clock on Friday I sprinted home with the same anticipation.

And what a place home was. To afford living in Santa Barbara with entry-level salaries, this meant packing five guys into a small three-bedroom house on the outskirts of town. All of us college friends, we played video games at night, ironed our shirts in the mornings, then spent our days perfecting *cubicle work* — the art of spreading one hour of actual work to fill an entire day.

Neither kids nor adults, somewhere between growing and grown, we were playing an extended game of make-believe that we were becoming full-functioning adults. I expected to hear our parents yelling to come home for dinner. But they just kept letting us play.

And Santa Barbara is an amazing, strange place to try to become an adult. It's where the Oprahs of the world live when they need a break from reality. The weather, the shops, the beaches, and the attractiveness of the men and women alike make it feel like you're either in a sci-fi movie where people are going to start growing extra limbs laced with precious metals, or God literally set up Santa Barbara as Plan B if heaven reached capacity.

Even the homeless people in Santa Barbara had a little extra swagger and a head shot in their shopping cart.

The house we rented was nothing extraordinary, but it did have an orange tree and a hot tub in the back. So you didn't hear any of us complaining. Unless of course you got some strange rash from the hot tub that we diligently cleaned about once a year — in a good year.

With five guys in one house, each day you frequented the kitchen or the bathroom was like playing a game of "Will This Be the Most Disgusting Experience of my Life?" Every three months we were implementing some new cleaning scheme or chore chart, which was honored for about three weeks until we threw a Fourth of July party that we'd clean up from sometime around Christmas.

The refrigerator was the fiercest battleground of them all. Trying to find your food in the refrigerator was like Indiana Jones searching for the Holy Grail — dangerous and exciting, with a chance of spotting a giant rodent of unusual aptitude.

The joys of bachelor, groan-up, adult life.

At the house I shared a cozy room with Rob, sleeping on a bunk bed we had happened to commandeer from a dorm room at our now former school. Heck, we were going to be paying them back until we were fifty-seven and a half years old, so we figured a "donated" bunk bed was the least they could do. Put it on our tab if you want to.

Rob was the best friend money couldn't buy. As I mentioned before, Rob started out his illustrious career packing nutcrackers, then worked at the Boob Factory, and was now an IT specialist at a software company.

And if there were a contest for most social IT guy in the world, Rob would've been the judge now after winning the thing ten years in a row.

I'd never known anyone more dedicated to hanging out than Rob. He would sacrifice sleep, a meal, grades, and his job for one more video game or round of volleyball. With an infectious laugh, the heart of a human golden retriever, and a round stomach that he would play like a drum on a nightly basis — quite beautifully, I might add (YouTube can confirm this) — Rob was a guy you just wanted around.

And even if you didn't, he'd probably show up anyway.

Most nights before we went to sleep, Rob and I would lie in our respective top and bottom bunks talking, the dark granting us the freedom to share our secrets like brothers who hoped their parents wouldn't hear them whispering well past bedtime.

We were both wrestling with the same nagging fear that our lives were turning out nothing like we hoped. We felt like there was something more; we just had no idea what it was or how to get there.

We were both plagued with the same questions; we just began to answer them in very different ways.

The Crew

If you're going to have a house full of guys, it's pretty much a rule of thumb that you have to partner with a house full of girls to become "your crew" (and force you to clean the filthy place once in a while). The group of girls we spent most of our time with were fun, cute, and all somehow under five foot two.

In this group of girls was Mary, one of my closest girl friends from college. Mary had sandy-blonde hair, with a smile that could have gone on one of those big posters on the dentist wall that make you feel self-conscious about your own teeth. I liked her. I had fun with her. I could tell Mary things I couldn't even tell Rob.

Yet, every time I stepped up to the "let's cuddle with each other and watch *When Harry Met Sally*" line, I'd back away slowly, hoping no one would notice I was there. We even had "The Talk" one night, both of us admitting that taking our relationship farther had crossed our collective minds. Yet I didn't, I *couldn't*, date her. We'd never kissed. We'd never crossed any sort of line, and I was dead set on keeping it that way.

Why? Honestly, I wasn't quite sure. But I don't think it was a problem of liking her. I think it was a problem of liking her too much and not wanting to lose her when it didn't work out.

I desperately wanted to be in a relationship, while simultaneously not wanting to touch one with a thousand-foot pole. I wanted the security of someone else, while my insecurities pushed everyone away.

I was desperate for a relationship to bring stability to my unstable world. Yet the rocking waves made jumping to that boat feel impossible. Sure, I could leap. But instead of making it, I was sure I'd slam my head on the side rail and end up knocked unconscious in the ocean. And going to my watery grave does not even crack my top ten ways I hope to die.

I wanted a girlfriend like I wanted a thriving career — having either one would mean I was one step closer to home, with at least something braggable to take pictures of for Instagram. And something exciting to tell my parents so they could stop pinning all their hopes on their dog's future instead of mine.

Yet both a good career and a healthy relationship felt like unidentified flying objects that I couldn't quite take a picture of. If finding a thriving career felt like the impossible dream, finding a healthy relationship felt like successfully landing on Mars. Or Venus. Depending on your rocket.

On paper, dating Mary seemed like a smart move. But even though I didn't truly understand the questions going on inside of me, I knew bringing someone else into the equation wasn't the answer. Because when I wasn't hanging out at the house with Rob or with Mary, I was beginning to find my way into the night. And I didn't want to bring either one of them with me.

Collaborating with Coworkers

There was a Thursday night when three coworkers, my buddy named Chase and two female coworkers, decided to head out together after work. Being a twentysomething in an office feels like being an actor with a small part in an off-Broadway play. Once five o'clock hit, we wanted to see what we were really like offstage.

And as the night progressed, and so with it the drinks, sitting in a tight, dark, crowded bar blaring with live music, somehow my lips just happened to find rest on the lips of my female coworker.

Sure, the next day was a little awkward when I was handing her files instead of a drink. But we were paid actors. And we were good at our job. So good we rehearsed the same scene a few more times. What can I say? We were passionate about our craft.

Dream Come True

On another night out, I couldn't believe my luck running into Cynthia, a girl I'd had a crush on since we were college sophomores. She was like that 1950s cheerleader in high school whose picture could be found in the yearbook under the award "Super-Duper Cute."

Cynthia must have taught "Flirting 101" at the local community college, because she had the incredible knack for making any guy believe she was into them when that was far from the truth. Something I knew all too well.

I'd pursued her my entire junior year only to be categorized as her "really good friend whom she loved to talk to about her ex-boyfriend," so things never quite progressed like I hoped they would. But that night it was different. We were talking and laughing. Then drinking and dancing. Then to my amazed disbelief, kissing, our bodies pressed together with the beat of the song.

As we kissed, I remember thinking I still didn't mean anything to her. Nothing had changed. But I loved the realization that now she didn't mean anything to me either. We were entering a simple unspoken transaction, granting us both something we wanted while costing us nothing. Or at least nothing we could see.

I loved the comfort of these new relationships. They didn't require anything of me. Like playing a video game, I could simply press Reset when things got too complicated.

Like a Vegas hypnotist, alcohol gave us all the freedom to act like idiots. Then once daylight snapped its fingers, we could simply pretend none of our actions really happened.

Then we signed up again for tomorrow night's show.

Alcohol was the best wingman money could buy. I just forgot that, strangely, at night's end, it doesn't usually have your best interests in mind.

CHAPTER FIVE

MY OWN PERSONAL NAZI

It was a crisp fall day in October (which in Santa Barbara means sixty-eight degrees instead of the usual seventy-five) when our house decided it was high time to do our manly duty and throw a BBQ/Drinking Game Party Extravaganza. Our house was a central point for many different groups of friends, and that night, with the lure of free meat and alcohol, everyone showed up like twentysomething stray cats.

And of course, our usual crew was there, my best girl friend Mary wearing her fitted flannel shirt, extremely well-fitting jeans, and brown leather boots that could make any man yell, "Giddyup."

Before I went up to say hello, I just watched her for a minute laughing and telling a story to friends. She turned toward me as she smirked. I walked up and gave her a big hug that lasted a few seconds longer than planned, my nose refusing to leave the fragrance coming from her hair.

"Wow, you look great tonight." I couldn't hold it back if I wanted to.

"Well, thank you very much." Mary smiled as our eyes stayed locked.

I should've realized right there that, *Houston, we have an "Apollo is going to crash into the White House"* problem.

Let the Games Begin!

With the meat grilling and drinking games in full throttle, I was "forced" to play and lose three consecutive times, chugging drinks with the ease of an alcoholic grizzly bear. Then during drinking game intermissions, I was "forced" to throw in some shots of Jaeger to pass the time. Within one very productive hour, I was really going, or coming, or something. I don't really remember, because I was drunk.

As I walked inside to give my liver a breather, lo and behold, Mary was lying by herself in the giant Lovesack in the middle of the living room, looking like she was trying to nurse off a few drinking games herself. Perfect timing. I plopped down next to her, the sides of our bodies touching from head to toe as we looked up at the ceiling.

We laughed and flirted, our hands casually finding themselves quite at home in each other's. I whispered in her ear, and she returned the gesture. I don't know how long we stayed there, but if there was a party going on around us, we were oblivious.

They didn't call it a Lovesack for nothing.

Concerned

Rob was beginning to worry about me, this much I knew. Not just on this night, but all nights. I was beginning to go out without him often and "forgetting" to invite him along. Rob, just because of the good guy he was, was a reminder of what I was doing wrong. And I didn't want that note left on my fridge.

As the party ended, about ten of us decided the night was far from over, Mary and I included, so we headed to a karaoke bar down the street. Rob went as well — (1) because if people were still hanging out, it was against Rob's religion to let that happen without him, and (2) I'm pretty sure he came to keep an eye on me.

At the karaoke bar, more drinks commenced as Mary and I continued to play the part. The soft touch of a hand, the lingering arm around the back — all were saying more than our words ever did before.

As the girls went to the restroom before we went back to our house, Rob pulled me aside.

"Paul, you need to stop this right now."

"Stop what?" I said, acting the role of surprised bystander.

"Paul, you're leading her on. And if you don't stop now, someone's going to get hurt."

"Thanks, *Mooommmm*," I said, with dripping sarcasm, like I was thirteen again. "We're grown-ups now. I can make my own grown-up decisions."

"Paul, you're going to regret this."

"Worry about yourself." There was little room for wisdom in the direction I was headed.

Homeward Bound

As our car pulled up to the house, Rob's words repeated over and over in my head, and as we stepped into the house, my last little bit of reason made a valiant last stand. I needed to get to bed, alone, before reason could be sabotaged.

I quickly said my good-byes, told Mary I would call her tomorrow, and escaped toward my room like a convict running to get *behind* closed doors. Mary's face did not hide her surprise as she most likely expected an end to the night slightly different than this, but sleep was the only thing that could save me now.

I bounced from wall to wall like a cross-eyed bumper car

driver. Bed was the only answer I could think of. I did not care about making out, anyone's feelings, throwing up, brushing my teeth, taking off my clothes, nothing. Bed and only bed. Get me in bed.

Bed. Bed. Bed. Bed. Bed. *Beeeeeeeddddd.*

I entered my room, and in one last drunk push to the finish line, I half ran, half fell into sleep.

The night was over.

Sure, I drank way too much. Sure, I'd led Mary on, but maybe things could still be salvaged. I did not completely ruin my relationship with her, and for that I smiled, patting myself on the back. In a passed-out, drunk fashion, where you really pat your forehead, thinking it's your back.

I could escape into sleep. Tomorrow always grants us the possibility of another do-over.

But then thirty seconds or thirty minutes later (I'm not sure), lo and behold, I woke up to a Mary-shaped person crawling into my bed.

Now dang it; that's just not fair! The whistle had blown, the game was over, and here she is still playing! I looked to the ref to throw her out of my room with a game misconduct, but alas, no call.

Like a car driving on black ice, even when I thought I'd gained control, I was still spinning around.

And with enough alcohol in my system to kill a raccoon — even a sizeable, scrappy one who was the head of the neighborhood raccoon pack — the act we'd been dancing around for years was nothing but blurred and uncomfortable. Mainly because there is little room for enjoyment when you're concentrating with every muscle, bone, and ligament in your body not to throw up in another person's mouth. For their sake, of course, but also because it is a good rule of thumb that if you throw up in someone else's mouth, they are bound to reciprocate the favor.

Then you're in a real pickle.

The moment we'd been practicing and preparing for for years, at best receiving a 5.5 out of 10 — maybe a 6 if the Russian judge had been bribed.

After about thirty seconds or thirty minutes (still not sure), one of Mary's friends finally came in to grab her out of my bed like she was pulling her out of a burning car wreck. Which wasn't too far from the truth.

No Turning Back

No Magic 8 Ball was needed to reveal that Mary's and my relationship would never be the same, and neither was my relationship with our "crew" of girls. I tried to casually remind everyone that it was she who came into my bed and not the other way around. But I knew it was a technicality that was going to fail to get me off scot-free.

You hurt one girl in a group of friends, and whenever you enter the room, the rest of them try to break your arm with their eyes.

Mary and I tried to talk it through a week later when the make-out dust had settled, but like mold, once it's there it's hard to get rid of. We tried to find a way where we could go back to normal, but after just completing a major rewrite, how could we expect to act the same parts?

Band of Brothers

Later that week, Rob came into our room and found me sitting on our floor, which hadn't been vacuumed since Clinton was president, just staring at the wall like a certified crazy person. I had no idea where to go for answers, so staring at nothing seemed like a good place to start.

We stayed up late that night talking from bottom bunk to top, like we'd done many times before. I tried to tell him, and myself, why I was struggling so bad. I knew I was trying to escape, but from what? What was going on with me?

I don't think my friends' doing great things is what's really bothering me, or that most of my life is now spent in "Templand" encased in five-foot rainy-gray walls. I mean, that doesn't help, but while watching *Band of Brothers* earlier that night, I started to understand.

Band of Brothers is the amazing HBO miniseries that Steven Spielberg and Tom Hanks did about the Easy Company paratroopers, some of the toughest, most heralded men of World War II. They went through the most grueling training, fought in the nastiest battles, and watched friend after friend die.

I could clearly see that what these soldiers went through was horrendous. Even if one were to escape with his life, that guy would never fully heal. But as I talked to Rob that night, I told him I envied those soldiers. *Why?* I envied them because they were in a battle against a *tangible enemy*. There across a field was a group of Germans. Germans were bad. Germans were the enemy. Your job was to kill them. You had objectives. You had weapons. You had an enemy you could see, touch, shoot, and, more importantly, kill. I wish I had my own personal Nazi. I wanted a tangible enemy right in front of me that I could see, touch, and kick in the nuts.

I feel like I'm fighting in a war that's less like WWII and more like Vietnam. I'm fighting an enemy I can't see, with an objective

I don't understand, expecting anything and everything to kill me at any second.

Where's my Great War? My Great Cause? I have a bachelor's degree in communication studies and a car payment. I don't think Steven Spielberg will do a miniseries about that.

The anxiety I feel would make much more sense if there were a war. Depression would be reasonable if I had it bad. I have a job. I have food. I have a bed to sleep on. I live in beautiful Santa Barbara amongst the wealthiest people in the world. What do I have to complain about?

Nothing. And the fact that I have no reason to be depressed is what depresses me more than anything else.

I couldn't shake this unshakable feeling that my life had no purpose. Leading up to this point my life had been so structured. Now I feel lost in an abyss of ambiguity. I thrived in a tight stairwell lined with syllabi, curfews, rules, Bible verses, and prompts to just keep taking that next step. Keep climbing higher. Because after college, you'd open up that door at the top and you'd *arrive*. At what, who knew, but you were pretty sure it entailed ample amounts of success and purpose, making all the steps you took to get there completely worth it.

But when we got to the top, swung open the door, and yelled "Here I am!" no one was there to even pretend to care. No one was waiting to greet us and usher us to our place in the world.

Instead, we opened the door and found ourselves back in the basement. Barely lit, numerous locked doors — and when we make it to the end of the hall, we're met by a mid-level manager with a wicked comb-over, who laughs in the face of our résumé like it's some sort of stand-up comedy routine.

It was time to explore in faith, but all I felt was fear. I'm living without definition now, blank white walls creating an empty space, and I don't know how, or what, to paint. I guess all along I had been looking for another formula, and instead I was given the opportunity to create something new. Why was I so afraid to pick up my brush?

Like most nights, Rob and I talked without coming to any conclusions. But to simply be honest with someone else who actually understood was like finding an ally in the midst of the war. Neither of us was sure what we were fighting or how we would escape, but just looking over and seeing someone in the bunker with me was enough to help me fall asleep.

CHAPTER SIX

FIRE
ESCAPE
PLAN

After the debacle with Mary, I thought I'd come back to who I was. Whatever that meant. I wanted to stop, change directions, and walk down a lit path. Instead, I just ran faster down the same dark one.

Anxiety felt like a sumo wrestler sitting across my chest. No matter how far I ran, I couldn't seem to shake my three dogs named *Discouragement, Depression,* and *Despair.* Even when I escaped deep into the night, these dogs were hot on my trail. They knew my scent too well.

I had believed my whole life that my life was meant for something more. That crumbling belief was now the dry rot fueling the flames.

So I began my fire escape plan. Girls had burned me so many times before; why not look to them for safety? An uncontrollable fire was raging; why not douse it with massive amounts of alcohol? Needless to say, I didn't fare well in chemistry class.

Yet no matter how far I ran the night before, each morning was a realization that this *escape* was becoming inescapable.

Out of desperation, I crawled to church one morning, a place I'd been avoiding for years. But as the pastor did his hallelujah dance across the stage, the crowd raising their hands in the synchronized spirit like some sort of heavenly wave, my hands couldn't move toward God. I felt like a stranger, out of place amongst such bright hallelujahs.

I slipped out the back before they could ask me to leave.

Road Trip Truth

It's a scientific fact that 87.3 percent of all confused twenty-somethings believe a road trip will fix everything. I was definitely in the majority.

So when some acquaintances proposed to pile in a few cars we weren't sure could make it out of town, let alone up the California coast, I agreed without hesitation. It was a chance to escape the dark corners and the holy pews, the night as well as the day. I was going with a group I barely knew, but familiarity was the last thing I wanted.

As we headed up the coast, I sat in the backseat, looking across the blue waters of the Pacific that I used to shout praises over. The water looked so calm. This unending canvas of blue, untouched and unchanging. My forehead against the side glass of a Honda, I swore I would change. I would call it quits. Enough was enough. Whatever I was doing wasn't working. I would escape this escape. This time I meant it.

Night number one of the trip I was a new, changed man.

Night number two, I was back. My transformation lasted about seventeen hours. Apparently when my conscience and alcohol battled each other in a game of King of the Hill, I didn't even stand a chance.

There was a girl. There was a bar scavenger hunt. There was a contest involving Irish Car Bombs. There was ... the short synopsis of my life.

As this girl and I drank, and drank, then danced, then stole away from all the curious eyes, I could almost hold the pain she was carrying with her. It was her accessory, more real than her pleather purse.

I'm sure she had a beauty about her that she didn't even

understand. She had a vision for her life that somehow became blurry long ago. But her pain was as apparent as her red lipstick.

Why was I surprised? Of course she was hurting. Why else would she be sneaking away with *me*? Wounded people love bleeding on each other.

We partook in some nightly activity, in some alley, outside of some bar, in some town. I was there, but not. Feeling, yet numb. Then she did a strange thing. She pulled away and looked directly at me.

Why was she looking me in the eyes? Didn't she know the rules?

She studied my face like she was trying to read the small print. I felt sick, yet strangely relieved. *Maybe I'd really been seen?* Someone, somehow, really saw the truth. I held my breath as she leaned in and whispered.

"I don't believe in love at first sight, but I do believe in my gut. And my gut's telling me that this could be something really, *really* special."

Apparently the truth was forever elusive.

Having just learned my name yesterday, she went on to carefully present her case why we should get married, have 2.4 kids, live in an off-white house, and own a dog named Mittens, or something like that. She kept talking and talking, word after word coming from her mouth like gnats I wanted to slap away. As her appeal for "love at first sight" continued, so did my disgust.

It wasn't disgust for her and her hope for one day owning a dog named Mittens; it was a disgust that somehow her dreams were here in this alley with me, her heart being drunkenly poured out next to a dumpster.

It was a disgust that I was here again, sitting on this curb, on this night, with this girl, deceiving yet another on this long list strewn with casualties. Myself included.

While she kept talking, something strange began to happen. I literally felt like I was rising out of my body as though gravity had forgotten its daily responsibilities. I hovered over this back-alley scene, having one of those real and honest appraisals. Like glancing in a mirror without realizing at first it's your own reflection.

There *this guy* was. Slumped over, sitting on a curb, head almost in his lap, looking like an old ragged dog. I felt sorry for him. I wanted to help him out, give him a hand up, but I didn't know how.

This hovering lasted about ten seconds before, unfortunately, I had to enter back into the reflection. Reality was the curb. Reality was the dumpster. Reality was me. Or, better put, this version of me.

She continued to talk, but all I could hear was, *Who the hell have I become?*

Over and over and over and over.

And there listening to some stranger tell me I was *her* answer, how together we could lick each other's wounds until neither one of us was bleeding anymore, I rolled my eyes back and fell headfirst into the sidewalk. A fall unbroken by hands. A fall caused more from hopelessness than being drunk. Her only choice now — to run and get help.

Head resting on a concrete curb, face grafted with pebbles, alone on a sidewalk, there I lay. *How did I get here? How did I let this happen?*

Well, I guess it didn't just happen. It took place a long time ago.

It happened with the daily grind. With the monotony of everyday life. With my fire escape that led me deeper into the flames.

The road to faith lost is full of small, "who gives a crap?" compromises.

I rolled over on my back and looked up at the sky. If the moon was out, I couldn't see it. The sky was black. Unknowing. Unending.

CHAPTER SEVEN

The next morning, as all my collective hangovers wore off, I hoped the pain would fade as well. But it didn't. Like a red wine stain on white carpet, it wasn't going anywhere. Alcohol, my only ally, turned tail and ran out of my blood system. Leaving me to face the fire, *mano a mano*.

I was unable to feel normal — whatever *normal* meant — any longer. I racked my brain to remember who I was, but I had amnesia. For the rest of the day I tried everything I could to produce some feelings of peace, even if they were forced. I'd have accepted a fake treaty over the pain of this war any day.

It wasn't that I'd gotten drunk again, or that there was another random girl, or that my forehead was cut where I had unceremoniously introduced it to a concrete curb. It wasn't any of those things — it was all of them. It wasn't one night. It wasn't the last six months, or year, or five years. No, it was my whole life.

I had my finger on a big red button and kept pushing it like a doorbell, hoping someone would come to help. Instead, I just kept standing there, self-destructing.

Jail Cell

Toward the end of the day, we road trippers were staying at the house of a friend's first cousin's girlfriend when I felt like the room I was in was closing in on me. I could hear the lock turning, the length of my sentence in this dark and dingy place unending.

I needed out — out of the room, out of the house, out of my skin, out into the night. I needed a real escape.

I jerked open the door to the house and just started sprinting. If I were in a reality show, this would be the scene where I did everything I could to escape the cameras.

I didn't know where I was running to, but I knew what I was running from — myself and God. I'd thrown me and God in the hall closet, under coats and behind the vacuum, hoping never to see either of them again. Sometimes I would hear God banging on the door. Or I'd see myself sneaking around the kitchen trying to get something to eat. But I was able to contain the two pretty well. Until that night.

As I booked it across California suburbia, block after block after block — fists pumping frantically — I could feel someone or something following me.

I sprinted full bore, like a thief running in front of an approaching squad car. But I could not shake the force behind me. As I ran, I could literally hear echoing all around me Sufjan Stevens's drenching refrain from "Seven Swans":

> *He will take you.*
> *If you run, he will chase you.*
> *He will take you.*
> *If you run, he will chase you.*
> *'Cause he is the Lord, he is the Lord, he is the Lord.**

Then it happened. The running, the sprinting, the staggering — all came to a skidding stop. I went down. To the sidewalk. Again. This time to my knees.

Dropping to one's knees seems like a cliché thing to do

---

* "Seven Swans," lyrics by Sufjan Stevens. Used with permission of New Jerusalem Music.

in a rock-bottom moment. But when the weight of the world combines with the weight of your mistakes, there aren't many options but down on your face.

Ledge of Grace

There I lay, my cheek embedded with small pieces of sidewalk once again, but this time under different circumstances. I don't think I've ever seen someone weep graciously, and that night, I definitely was no exception. Tears fell like I was trying to clean the sidewalk with my face.

I've heard many people talk about the need to "surrender to God." It always seemed like a sappy phrase used by pastors before making an appeal for us to also "surrender our finances" to God, and, of course, to the church as well, for the new wing they're building and the 3D movie theater.

But for me that night, surrender was lying face-first on a suburban sidewalk. No longer pretending I had the answers. No longer pretending I even had the right questions. Surrender was prostrate, face on hard, cold concrete.

But as I fell that night, I learned that God gives us ledges of grace to land on. Ten, fifteen, twenty feet below. He won't let us fall all the way to our deaths. He'll give us checkpoints along the way.

So you crash onto his ledge. It's still painfully hard ground — you just fell a shorter distance to get there. You land broken, but still breathing.

I was searching for rock bottom; instead, I got a rocky ledge of grace.

Climb or Fall?

On that ledge I knew I had a choice: Do I stand, look up, and give the pain back to God? Ask him to be my fire escape this time? Or do I roll over the edge and simply continue my free fall, clutching my pain as the parachute that won't open?

Thomas Merton wrote, "It is better to find God on the threshold of despair than to risk our lives in a complacency that has never felt the need for forgiveness."* So according to a very smart monk named Thomas Merton, I was in a really good place. The threshold of despair. Awesome.

But on this threshold was there room for forgiveness? Was God bigger than my mistakes? Did his grace extend farther and higher than this ledge? Or was I left here on my own?

Chocolate

I don't know how long I lay there. It was long enough to feel self-conscious a couple of times, wondering what some lucky neighbor would do if she strolled down this sidewalk with her poodle. But as I contemplated my options, I felt something I hadn't in a long time. I couldn't quite put my finger on it, but I think it resembled hope.

I'd made a ton of horrible decisions. My life was a million miles from where I wanted it to be. But there was this small thing inside me that whispered, *I still care*. I'd cursed him, run from him, spat in his face. But God cared enough about me to let me crash down.

Tears lining my lips with salty surrender, I began to laugh. I

---

*Thomas Merton, *No Man Is an Island* (New York: Harcourt, 1955), 21.

wept out of overwhelming despair. I laughed out of subtle hope. A weird paradox, lying face-first on a suburban sidewalk.

I wish I could say I rose with all the answers. I wish I could say I woke my neighbors as I skipped home, singing at the top of my lungs about the love of Jesus.

No, I stood up in the kind of pain that smashing down onto sharp rocks after a free fall will give you. But unlike any other time in a long time, I stood up with a small sliver of hope. Like a lost boy in a war-ravaged land who just found a piece of rare chocolate.

Sure, there was still a war raging. But for the moment, I had chocolate.

SCANDALOUS LOVE

I know this whole grace thing is amazing, but it's awful too. Grace ruins us. It brings in a scalpel to surgically remove tumors without even putting us under.

Sure, not all grace is painful. There's grace that protects, nourishes, and propels forward. The grace trampoline bounces us to places we never thought imaginable. I love that kind of grace. It feels much more like the amazing kind.

Then there's the ledge of grace — the grace I experienced. It saves by breaking. It smacks you until you're red and tender, but says it's doing it out of love. And while that's probably true, you don't dare try to convince your butt.

But how much of that pain is actually coming from him, and how much from me? Grace doesn't hold a grudge. It says, "I know. I forgive. Let's move on." It holds out before me the promise of my do-over like a plate of freshly baked cookies.

But I wasn't about to let grace get me off the hook that easily. No way. Not after what I'd done. Because grace isn't cheap, right? No bites of warm cookies for me. I needed a strict diet of guilt, tasting less like chocolate and more like lemons mixed with asbestos.

I began slamming my head against the wall, hoping if I made myself bleed enough I could be counted worthy again. I needed to pay the price for each dirty little secret on my quite extensive laundry list.

It would take months for me to learn that my blood was just blood. Nothing more.

Unwanted Changes

I was ready for the uplifting, rock-bottom-to-mountaintop story to unfold, but it wasn't happening. Whoever was writing my story needed to take a couple lower-division creative writing classes.

Sure, on the outside I became healthier again. I stopped drinking. Stopped hooking up with random girls. Started reading the Bible again, an hour a day. Okay, more like ten minutes a day. Okay, five minutes. Okay, so I found my Bible again under my bed.

But my depression doubled. My anxiety tripled.

Hey, God, I'm back on that right religious track. Isn't it time to wave your magic wand and fix me?

Apparently God isn't a magic fairy.

I wanted him to heal me while I beat myself up; he wanted me to stop beating myself up so I could heal.

So grace did something radical. Something unconventional. Grace decided it was time I go to Wilmore, Kentucky.

Rough Week at Camp

I was working now as an admissions counselor for my alma mater. It wasn't my dream job, but it definitely could've been worse. As an office we took one trip together to the annual Christian Admissions Conference, this year being held at Asbury College in Kentucky. These conferences are like summer camp but for "professionals." The major difference is more lectures and less capture the flag. (We did have dodgeball, though.)

About a hundred twentysomethings were at this conference, many of them single, many keeping their eyes peeled for the catch of the week. By day four, the summer camp syndrome would take over, and every guy and gal had crushes on about fifteen eligible singles.

Not me, though. There was one girl there named Naomi, whom I had met once months before and had a gigantic crush on. But she was so far out of my league it would've been like a second grader trying out for the NFL. With her long black hair, big brown eyes, and perfect brown skin, she literally looked like Princess Jasmine. Unless I commandeered a magic genie, I was better left out on the street.

Plus, I was too busy walking around with my eyes to the ground, face shoved in my many past "accidents," to entertain any thought of a relationship.

The entire week all I wanted was to go home. Or to a monastery.

It has to be easier to right the ship at a monastery.

Love This Enemy?

I know we're supposed to love our worst enemy. But what if that enemy is you? Is there some sort of biblical escape clause then?

Parts of me I like. I like *Party Paul*, the guy who can tell stories to friends and get a laugh. When he's on his A game, I'm quite fond of him.

I like *Athletic Paul*, making a diving catch or spiking a volleyball. Sure, all five foot ten of his Italian frame only success-fully spikes about one out of fifteen volleyballs, but you'd better believe when he gets that one, he looks over at the girls playing next to him, fully expecting them to be staring in awe. (They are really good at pretending they don't notice, though.)

And *Friend Paul* — he's all right. He's not great when you really need answers or when you really need someone to cry with. That makes *Friend Paul* slightly uncomfortable. But he is good at cracking jokes to make you forget.

But *Paul Paul* … The man I am, with no costumes. Stripped of accolades, compliments, grades, laughs. Paul without any cool frills or features. The guy I have to carpool with every day to work. Frankly, I'm not a huge fan. Every morning I turn up the music really loud to let him know we won't be talking.

I'm slowly coming to understand that I disliked myself before all the grace. But now it was actually worse, because I could blame myself for needing *so much* grace. Now I had new memories of failing, of sinning. New ways to be guilty. New and exciting ways to be ashamed. A fun, rickety carousel I'd been spinning around on my whole life.

Here's a lesson I'm learning: Don't ever go into a major life transition if you don't like yourself. Don't even try it. Flunk your senior year so you'll have to stay. Extend your contract one more year at that job you don't like. Day by day, just work on liking yourself.

Because in major life transitions, those things called acco-lades, status, praise, titles — yeah, you're probably not going to be seeing those for a while. If you liked yourself based solely on "success," then you're going to dislike yourself based solely on all the failure.

Sardines

I had my bags packed a day and a half before we were supposed to leave the conference. Going to a monastery was still a possibility, but I'd searched for some on the Internet and couldn't find many choices. Monasteries don't seem to advertise much online.

So home sweet home it would be.

But around ten o'clock the night before we left, some admissions counselors got a game of sardines going as a last hoorah — the game where one person hides, then everybody else has to find him. Summer camp syndrome, officially taking control.

Scampering around campus with them sounded about as exciting as an accounting seminar. But it was either that or face myself alone in the room. So I chose sardines.

Wandering around, I did my typical feeling sorry for myself that I disliked myself so much. Then I disliked myself even more for feeling so sorry for myself.

If other people actually existed, I hadn't the faintest.

So with my head set in its downward position, I turned the corner of a building and ran smack-dab into another living person.

"Oh, sorry," she said.

"Yeah, me too; sorry," I said, looking up. As my eyes met her face, a short little gasp escaped from my mouth.

Oh, crap. Princess Jasmine.

Normally, I would have stuttered out an attempt at a joke. Like, "we've got to stop running into each other like this," while simultaneously sucking in my gut and flexing my arms a tad. But that night I wasn't in the mood. I turned and kept walking.

"Hey, have you looked over there?" she asked.

Did she just talk to me again? I think she did. Okay, I'm supposed to do something in this situation. I'm supposed to respond. Vowels, consonants, forming words. Say something, Paul, anything. She asked if I'd looked over there. Had I?

"Uhhh, no?" It was all I had. Apparently it was a good enough response because together we looked over there, and then looked over here. Then we walked around campus looking everywhere for about an hour.

Why this girl Naomi was talking to me I literally had no idea. But when you think she's "drop down to your knees and thank God for women" beautiful, you don't ask questions. You just hold on.

Her Confession

After walking and talking quite a while, having the usual, casual, semi-awkward conversation, she interrupted with something unexpected.

"Paul, can I confess something to you?"

Wow. *Her* confess to *me*? I had about a hundred things I could confess to her, but I wasn't about to open my big mouth. "Go ahead," I said.

"Well, a couple of friends and I made a bet this weekend. And the bet was who could kiss somebody first at the conference. And, well, I picked you as the person I would kiss. But the person I bet against just kissed someone, so I lost. So now I'm just telling you."

I'm pretty sure there's no decent response to a confession like that. Especially considering everything going on in my life. Luckily my A game kicked in.

"Uhhhh … okay," I responded.

"Sooooo ...," she replied.

"Sooooo ...," I replied back.

Our conversation had deteriorated to a "sooooo" standoff. *Sooooo* we just kept walking.

Here I am, coming off of a tailspin where I took all my pain to alcohol and girls.

Here I am, feeling completely unlikeable, talking to someone I really like.

Of course. It just makes sense.

That night turned out to be one of the most awkwardly amazing nights of my life. Two admissions counselors from competing schools in California, until 5:00 a.m., on a bench in the middle of Kentucky.

Here I was, trying desperately to right the ship, make sense of my life, and *not* kiss another random girl the first night. No alcohol in my system to guide my actions this time; all I had was me. And *Way over His Head Sober Paul* had no game, this much I knew.

Then here was Naomi, who, I'd later find out, was trying to do something rebellious for once in her life, breaking out of her comfort zone, hoping to kiss a random guy for the first time in her life.

It's moments like these when you realize life isn't a math formula where if you punch in the same numbers, you get the same answer.

Life is a Shakespeare sonnet. It's long. It's complicated. People tell you it's beautiful. And you'd probably agree with them if you could only understand a single word.

And at 5:00 a.m., after hours of great conversation and much internal debate, I finally leaned over and kissed her.

And it was ... *terrible*.

I mean awkwardly bad. I felt like I'd relapsed back to my eighth-grade self, kissing with all teeth and insecurities, trying to find my breath like a pug climbing a hill.

It was so bad that as I was pulling away, Naomi was already yawning. She then quickly announced it was time for her to go to bed.

I'd blown my chance. I knew it. I was going to be as memorable to her as the cafeteria enchiladas she had eaten earlier that week. Walking toward the dorm where she was staying, I knew I had to do something. Fast. Two steps away from her door something came over me. It was the act of a desperate man who knew he had only one chance. Without thought, premeditated plan, or time to call myself an idiot, I grabbed Naomi's arm, swung her toward me, and just freaking kissed her.

I was trying out for the lead role, and dang if I wasn't at least going to give the judges something to talk about.

I pulled away from the kiss, bid Naomi good night, and walked away. By the look in her eyes I'd either just sealed the deal or gotten myself a restraining order. I wasn't sure.

But as I walked back to my room I thanked God. Somehow, after all I'd done the last year leading up to this moment, a kiss without reservation might've somehow been in God's plans all along. Sweet, lovely grace.

Long Story Short

A couple of weeks later, this amazing woman named Naomi was dating despicable me. Apparently I had a magic genie after all.

Now I've heard many wise people say you should never get involved in a relationship as the answer to your problems. They couldn't be more right. But when you have a person you really like and respect wanting to talk to you on the phone as if you're someone worth his or her time, you either ...

   a. call them a liar and hang up

     or

   b. try to see what they see and just keep talking

     I chose b.

For the next few months, God and Naomi were in cahoots with each other. Determined to make me love my enemy again. Or at least make me ride with him to work without getting into a huge fight. Their plan was so obvious I almost wanted to laugh at the transparency of it all. But I didn't. Instead I just let them scheme. I was tired of throwing a mutiny against myself every time my ship set sail. And too faint from all the lost blood.

Naomi's faith was different from mine — honest and full of actual faith. Her days weren't laced in doubt. It was refreshing. Plus, she was as beautiful as the lead role, while simultaneously as quirky as the best friend played by a former member of *Saturday Night Live*.

She didn't shy away from calling out my "stuff" and asking me the questions she knew I was petrified to ask myself. There was no beating around the bush; instead she lit that bush on fire to see what I was trying to hide behind it.

Not Following the Rules

Naomi didn't fix all my problems. Not even close. Actually she was just the beginning of realizing how many problems I really had. Relationships force open our closet doors and reveal all the secrets we've been hiding behind the big coats and Christmas sweaters way in the back.

It didn't take long to realize my biggest problem: my constant belief that I had so many problems. I was drowning in self-imposed problems because I was a self-imposed failure. I wasn't doing a job I could brag about. I wasn't doing what I deemed as big and important. I sinned too much and was righteous too little. I was constantly blowing some standard, some image I had created.

I was a disappointment. And if I was disappointed, so was God. He had to be. He was more than aware I wasn't shaping up into the fine young man he'd hoped for. I kept waiting for him to smack me with that measuring stick I wasn't living up to and dangle me over the flames like a marshmallow at a campfire. No wonder I was always anxious.

But that night on his ledge of grace, I sensed he still loved me, and this threw me into a theological tailspin. He blessed me when I didn't deserve it. I never deserve it. But this time, without a doubt, instead of a graceful dive into the pool, I did the biggest belly flop of my life. I knew, because my stomach was still stinging and bright red.

And as I came out of the water expecting his look of disappointment, I received something different. A smile. Not a little smile, but ear to ear — as if I'd just done a dive worthy of a gold medal. He lifted me out of the pool, grabbed a towel, and wrapped it around my hurting body. He picked me up and started bragging about me to all his friends.

When I was lying belly flopped and broken on a suburban sidewalk, I yelled, "Help me."

That was it.

It was all he needed.

Will the Real God Please Stand?

That's the thing about God, the part of him that's dangerously close to demolishing my sick little cycle of guilt and insecurities. I'm realizing my frills and features don't matter to him. Whether I'm working in a cubicle or being a wallflower, alone in my room with a million questions, or onstage with what I think are the right answers, he stays the exact same. God isn't swayed by what I do or don't do. Whether I'm right or wrong. However many times I change colors to match the world around me, he'll stay the exact same. This doesn't give me carte blanche to sin however I please — just a complete do-over for every time I ask for help.

At an ancient well in Samaria, Jesus didn't see a wayward woman deserving to be condemned; he saw a person of beauty, inside and outside, who needed a second chance. Up in the branches of a sycamore-fig tree, Jesus didn't see a corrupt tax collector who'd ripped people off; he saw an insecure man looking for acceptance and yelled up to him in front of a crowd, "You. Me. Dinner. Tonight. You're cooking. What do you say?"

God gives my identity permanence. He doesn't distinguish between *Party Paul* and *Insecure Paul*. *Athletic Paul* and *Depressed Paul* can join hands together in the same circle and do the same dance and sing the same song, because they're all one and the same child to him.

God's love doesn't need me to win any gold medals before he will wrap my hurting body in a big, warm towel.

Runaway Children

We're all the prodigal son or daughter in various shapes and forms. Disowning, rebelling, bathing in muck at times, with varying degrees of success and failure. You can spit in his face, take off to Vegas, lie, cheat, steal, murder. Name any sin; it's all been done before.

Or maybe we're the older brother or sister. On the outside, all buttoned up. Doing and saying all the right things. But on the inside, cold and empty, seething with resentment, mad at your dad and furious with the world. Maybe you've been bitterly waiting on God to reward all your good efforts with the fattened calf, angry that he seemingly failed to comply. When all along God simply wanted you to stop and enjoy with him the unfathomable truth that "it's been yours" all along.

But the moment you come back (or come to yourself), the moment you cry, "Please forgive me" — no matter how dirty, how sinful, how shameful, how smug and self-righteous — he's picking you up in his arms, spinning you around till you feel sick, laughing and crying so ferociously that the neighbors come outside to see what all the noise is about.

I don't comprehend how anyone can love in that manner. It's the definition of radical, of countercultural. Truly so unconditional that it's borderline scandalous. A love that makes neighbors stare with furrowed brows of disbelief and disgust at a filthy son deserving so little being spun around by a Father deserving so much.

Extremely Easy, Extremely Hard

Simply put, I don't earn my identity or earn his love; I simply accept.

This was a huge, monumental shift in my religious thinking, something that had pervasive power to change how I saw him and myself. All I do is simply stop putting conditions on something that by its very nature cannot have any.

His grace would be a different word entirely if I actually deserved it. His love would lose its soul if I could make it have limitations. Every time we try to give his love an "if" or "but," we dam up something that was meant to flow, leaving us with a stagnant, reeking pond of scum and muck to wade through and wonder why we feel so sick. His grace simply wants to wash it all downstream.

I thought I could tell God something about my identity with guilt. With all my bitterness and pain, I could change the way he thought of me. But I'm slowly realizing I gave myself way too much credit.

He doesn't love like us; he loves like him.

CHAPTER NINE

SANDBOX DREAMS

can understand now why people freak out when they hit forty. The birthday cake comes out shining like an over-decorated Christmas tree, and they realize they're halfway done with the race they barely knew they started.

For me, time began to march now with steady consistency. I was doing well at my job. I mean, I wasn't going to be named admissions counselor of the year or anything (there actually is such an award; and no, I didn't win), but I could hold my own. I could counsel those high school kids like they've never been counseled before.

I eased back into my job and set life to cruise control. The fire started to grow dim as my life wasn't really in transition any longer. It was just life again.

No more pesky dreams or thoughts of changing the world. I'd learned my lesson. In the "real world," big dreams just didn't fit in. It's much easier to let them mosey on down the road than to keep running after them, begging them to come back, prom-ising to use them really soon, then watching them sit there bored to tears and checking their watch.

Dreams were for those days spent playing in the sandbox. They were to be kept in storage with the Superman cape and princess tiara. In the real world, you settled. That's just the way it was. Dreams were dangerous reminders of something you'll never have. And the quicker you get over them, the quicker you become a useful, faithful member of adulthood.

But then, back at a bar, of all places, a random stranger had to bust in and mess up a good thing.

Ice Cube Focus

I was sitting on a stool, waiting for friends to join me for dinner. The place was packed, people sitting so close together I could feel the Tic Tacs in my neighbor's pocket.

When strangers are that close, it's a little awkward if you don't at least say a cursory hello. Plus, the fellow sitting next to me was doing the "I'll stare at you without blinking for as long as it takes for you to look my way," so after a five-minute battle where I pretended I was completely entranced by the women's basketball game with no sound, I finally turned toward him.

His name was Chris, and he lived at the hotel two miles down the road. About five foot six with unkempt hair beginning to turn gray and a flannel shirt halfway tucked in, he told me he walked to this bar every night, drank the same drink (in multiples of four, it smelled), and then walked back to his hotel home.

Chris said that when he was growing up, he was always good at computers and never really tried anything else. So he took a job right out of high school at a big computer company. After two years, he started getting the itch to leave. He was taking in a decent paycheck, but what he really wanted was to go after his dreams.

"But I couldn't leave," he told me, his eyes fixed on the ice cubes swimming in his glass as if they were threatening him to stay on script. "I hated staring at the computer screen all day. I hated that I never spoke all day to one living person. But the money was just too good. So I stayed. For fifteen years. And quite frankly, I couldn't take it anymore. So I quit. I can get that job back in a heartbeat if I want. But I can't live like that. Not anymore. So now I'm just living like this."

At this point I had to tell him my story. How I was finally getting comfortable in my job. How I was thinking about letting my dreams retire, kind of like he did.

He interrupted me, speaking with enough alcohol on his breath and red in his eyes that I had to listen.

"You're so young. Why settle now? I'm telling you, you'll regret it. Don't let the paycheck and comfort make the decision for you."

Of course a random guy at a random bar has to tell me this. Right when there's talk of a promotion and a big pay hike at my job. Right when life has become doable (though dull). Manageable again (and very mundane).

I don't even remember the dinner with my friends that evening. But I can't forget that man's eyes. Eyes that had seen deep into his drink and, quite frankly, didn't like what they saw.

Still Not Convinced

Following your dreams seems well and good. Idealistic enough to be a tad exciting. But as I seriously think about chasing dreams and possibly doing the whole job hunt again — and possibly, gasp, going to another temp agency, if need be — a feeling grows in the deep parts of me. I don't know how to describe it exactly. If I had to convey it in a single sentiment, it would be, *Ohhh, crap!*

Fear plagued me. Like moths on winter clothes in the attic, fear gnawed, chewed, and destroyed my courage. Fear had gripped me when I left college, and now, years out, it still had me in its clutch. But then while I was watching TV, *Joe Versus the Volcano*, of all things, stepped in.

Giant luggage, the Waponi, and a brain cloud. Remember this cinematic gem? Right after Joe (Tom Hanks) finds out he's about to die, he decides to leave his lousy job of gray concrete walls and fluorescent lights. He walks out the door with guns blazing against his terrible boss, wrapping it up in these words that have forever stuck with me: "I've been too chicken-shit afraid to live my life, so I sold it to you for three hundred freaking dollars a week!"

Who would have thought that *Joe Versus the Volcano* could make me seriously contemplate my life? But when you hear someone describe the way you're living as chicken excrement, it makes you take notice, no matter who's saying it.

I don't want my life to become an excuse. I don't want to be a forty-year-old crisis (like my friend at the bar) who realizes too late the truth: I'm miserable because I never took a chance.

Fear is a liar. It makes life seem impossible, overwhelming, something to be drowned out instead of lived. Fear is always there, swimming right under the surface, ready to latch on like a giant squid the moment we fall into the water.

Fear tells us, "This is far enough; start building right here," when we're two hundred miles shy of the destination we set out for.

Fear makes self-preservation a top priority. It makes "don't get hurt" the rule to live by. But our instinct for self-preservation will get us killed — a long, slow death. We'll sit there enduring drips of water falling on our forehead, one after another, day after day, until we snap and throw our computer through our boss's window and wear nothing else but Hawaiian shirts for a month. And I mean *nothing* else.

Sydney J. Harris wrote, "Regret for the things we did can be tempered by time; it is regret for the things we did not do that is inconsolable."*

I don't want to regret that I never took a big enough chance to regret anything whatsoever. You ease fear by doing it afraid. Then the next time, the fear is a little less frightening.

If you're afraid, do it anyway.

Personalized Scroll

I realize now that for years I wanted a dove to fly down with a scroll in its beak and drop it into my hand, tipping its little dove hat and saying, "Good day, sir," like a friendly 1950s mailman. I'd open the scroll and read God's handwritten, detailed map showing my step-by-step progression for the next fifty years.

Someone must have shot that dove because I still haven't seen it.

Maybe God's plans aren't something I need to wait to discover. Maybe I'm not supposed to view life as a confusing treasure map where if I take one wrong turn, I'll never find that chest full of gold and instead end up a wench serving drinks at the Hungry Margarita.

Maybe it's simpler than that? More practical and straightforward. Maybe I've already been given his plans. Maybe they have to do with what's stirring in my heart, those small urges that say, "I need to try this."

"Take delight in the LORD, and he will give you the desires of your heart" (Psalm 37:4). Maybe the dreams within our hearts, the ideas that quicken our pulse — maybe they are there for a

---

*Sydney J. Harris, *Strictly Personal* (Chicago: Regnery, 1953), 220.

reason. He created us, so when we discount what gets us excited, are we not just discounting the way he designed us?

I've cried for my life to line up with this abstract idea of his plans, like he's a father who has me locked up in a dark room. But maybe his plans have been within me this whole time. I know my heart's tainted. But I also know I'm not a mistake. My talents, abilities, and dreams are not mistakes either.

One way or another, I don't think God wants me to let suffocating fear make the final call. His plans don't play second fiddle to my own doubts and apprehensions, which try to say that sitting on the couch playing video games is a perfect way to spend my life.

Or that being chicken excrement is fine and dandy, as long as I'm getting paid well enough.

I don't think I should settle in a home I shouldn't be living in. I think it's right for me to say I don't want to be at a bar twenty years from now, staring at my drink as I tell some kid not to end up like me.

I want to risk. I *need* to risk. Sure, there will be times when I fall flat on my face, adding a scar to the rest of the collection. Sure, I will cringe when I read the next alumni magazine about those classmates who are the poster children of success.

But I don't want to worry about how I'll look; I want to worry about whether or not I'm living my life on purpose.

I want to create. I want to feel more. To step out in the rain, get down on my hands and knees, and look up. Hands and mouth opened wide.

I don't want to listen to music; I want to hear it. To feel it. To let it seep into my bones like a sponge. I don't want to just listen to a thousand songs; I want to truly sing just one.

I don't want my life to begin and end in mediocrity. I don't want to push paper in a cubicle and call it my lot; I want to do something significant.

But what if *significance* carries with it no accolades, billboards, or a feel-good "movie of the year"? What if I toil and sweat, and no one gives a rat's behind?

Will I have the courage to find meaning in the mundane? Will I be willing to dream in the big, while being faithful in the small? I'm working on dreaming again, but what about "faithful in the small"? What does that really mean? Coming out of college I was ready to dream big and then be faithful *in the big*. But my faith was like a newborn colt: put anything on my shoulders, and my little legs buckled. I wanted to carry a big worthy cause when the smallest of loads nearly broke my back. The "big" probably would've killed me.

If you're not secure with *less*, you will be crushed by *more*.

God saved my life by not giving me all those big things I cried out for. No matter how big my temper tantrum.

I thought I had faith. Turns out I didn't even understand the word.

CHAPTER TEN

MUSH,
GOD,
MUSH

"All right, God, let's do this. I'm ready to start acting again like you're really my Father instead of a crazy uncle I only invite over for major holidays. Show me the path I need to take. Put a spotlight on it. Blare some trumpets. I'm ready to move forward."

That was the gist of my prayer late one night as I did the six-hour drive from Sacramento to Santa Barbara. I do my best praying on road trips. In between static, Spanish radio stations, and lost cell phone signals, there's not much else to do but shout at God to show up.

Right at that moment, he did exactly that.

This may sound weird (and it was!), but I began seeing this extremely vivid picture in front of me, almost like it was being projected onto my windshield. The picture was so overwhelming that it was hard to see through. So at the next off-ramp, I pulled over. Either God was speaking, or I was five minutes from taking an unexpected exit off the highway, eyes firmly shut. Either way, pulling over seemed like a sensible idea.

The Drive-In Movie on My Windshield

I sat there and watched this vivid picture on my windshield. It was of a big, open valley at the edge of a forest. The setting sun was ten minutes from bidding its farewell. Winding through the valley was a long path, and I stood where it entered the forest.

The forest before me was thick, with massive pines so dense they seemed to form a giant wall. It grew darker every minute. The noises increased as friendly daylight creatures gave way to the night-shift bears and wolves.

I could tell I didn't want to go into this forest. But I had this feeling I was supposed to. I knew I'd walked far to get here, and there was no turning back. But I was scared.

As I stood there waiting for my courage to build, I looked to the left. I saw an old wooden wheelbarrow. Strange. So I did the only logical thing I could think of at the moment: I climbed in.

Sitting in the wheelbarrow, I started shouting to God a prayer I'd heard myself pray before: "Here I am, Lord. Send me!" That's all. Big smile across my face. I'd been faithful to get this far. Now it was his turn to move me onward.

There I sat, smiling, eager to see where I was going next. There I sat. And sat some more. I looked around a little. I thought about how hungry I was getting, and cold. There I stayed. An idiot in a wheelbarrow.

Sled-Dog God

As I prayed my prayer of "Here I am, Lord. Send me," I must have made God roll his eyes, put his head back, and sigh very deeply. If he does these sorts of things. I think he must, to stay sane when dealing with a bunch of people whom he loves but must want to just smack sometimes. Then I literally felt like he spoke to me in a very unchurchy kind of way.

"Paul, get out of the wheelbarrow. Lots of people have the faith to sit around and do nothing. That's not faith. I'm not going to push you around while you yell 'mush.' I'm not your freaking sled dog."

Faith?

It didn't take an intellectual or theological genius to recognize this picture of my self-defined faith. As I had entered the unknown, my "faith" was sitting still, waiting for God to get me through. Once I knew we were through the scary stuff, I'd be up and around again. Once I saw it all clearly laid out before me, I'd move. Once I was sure, I'd run full speed. Then I'd be the best, most faithful Christian this side of the Mississippi.

As I sat in my Honda at some random off-ramp in the middle of nowhere, I started laughing. What a bass-ackward definition of faith I had. I prayed and prayed for God to open doors for me, but I didn't even have the courage to walk close enough to see a door, let alone try the doorknob.

In my head, faith was theoretically sound but practically nonexistent. My faith was more the sitting-around-and-complaining kind. When God didn't instantly jump at my barked commands, I called him untrustworthy. He let me just sit there, so I called him a liar.

All this time I'd wanted a sled dog, not a savior.

Monster beneath My Bed

Later that week, wouldn't you know I'd get another definition of faith. Gosh, you pray for a year and hear nothing. Then *bam*, in one week God lays out a short novel for you to digest. Go figure.

This time the answer wasn't in my Honda, but under my bed. That's where I kept a gigantic bag filled with old folders and books, relics from my learning days. I pulled out that monster bag to see if it was still breathing.

I grabbed a notebook from "Reconciliation and Conflict Resolution," which was taught by one of my favorite professors, Dr. Mike Guiliano. I came across a note I'd starred and underlined so many times it instantly caught my attention. I remembered right away the day Dr. Guiliano said it because of how angry the comment had first made me. It was such a slap in the face.

The gist of his comments was that he thought students from our school were some of the least likely to make a big impact on this world. Because even though we were highly educated, with resources galore at our fingertips, our number one priority was comfort. We were obsessed with it. And it's impossible to change this world and remain comfortable.

In my notes I wrote, "I'm going to prove him wrong!"

Well, crap. Why didn't I just throw away all these dang notes when I had the chance? I guess my professors did tell me some pretty good stuff. I was just too smart to listen.

I realize now that when I left college and switched from being a campus twenty*something* to an unemployed twenty*nothing*, I cursed God because he'd removed what I'd really worshiped in the first place — the La-Z-Boy. He'd smashed my vision for the easy life by the pool — Mai Tais in one hand and a wad of hundred-dollar bills in the other.

All along I had worshiped God the Cruise Director, not God the Father. So when the all-you-can-eat buffet ran out of lobster, I started a mutiny before the ship could even leave port.

Definition?

So what is faith? I'd asked God for synonyms; he decided to show me antonyms instead. I got a slap in the face of what faith is *not*. Faith is *not* waiting for God to make life comfortable again while I sit in my deluxe wheelbarrow. Faith isn't pulling out my whip and trying to smack God into compliance. I wanted to be faithful to him only if I could completely control the direction he was taking me. When he wouldn't let me put the harness around his shoulders, I was hurt and offended and adamantly refused to move until he submitted to me.

Faith starts with that first step. When the fear in the back of my throat says, *I'm screwed*, faith lets me say, *Shut up*, and just keep walking. It doesn't matter that I have no idea what lies at steps two, eight, or fifty-five; it's up to me just to put one foot down and move forward.

First Baby Step

"Change is hell," Robert Quinn writes in his book *Deep Change*. "Yet not to change, to stay on the path of slow death, is also hell."* So let's see; I can either choose hell or more hell. I don't know if I like my options. But *slow death*, yeah, that doesn't sound very appealing.

However, the hell of deep change, Professor Quinn writes, is "the hero's journey." That has a nice ring to it. So why not embark down that path? At the very least, I can go out in a blaze of glory rather than smolder in slow-death monotony.

So, step number one: Leave my job. I know this. Because my job is comfortable, it's easy, and it's not what I am supposed to do. I don't want the job I never wanted to become that job I can't escape. Worse than a frustrating, demanding job is a job that demands nothing.

My professor was right. I've always been lured by comfort-

---

*Robert E. Quinn, *Deep Change: Discovering the Leader Within* (Hoboken, NJ: Wiley, 2010), 78.

able. It's been my cigarette — addictive and killing me with every puff.

Netflix benders and social media binges — our generation's drug of choice.

I need to quit comfortable before it's too late. Before I'm strung out on yet another "Season Seven," wondering why I just can't seem to find the time to pursue my dreams.

I'm taking that first step *into the wild*. If I'm not back in five minutes, feel free to give my wheelbarrow to the next deserving soul.

CHAPTER ELEVEN

I quit my job, and there I went. Los Angeles. Into the *wild*. A magical land of fairy-tale wishes and cotton candy clouds. (Though you can't really take a bite from any of the cotton candy clouds due to the high density of deadly toxins.)

LA is the Mecca for dreamers. It is the hub for those who have mocked reality in its face and left their comfortable lives to become one of the chosen few. We all grow up basking in the twinkling lights of Hollywood, so how can we not follow our hearts out west to live it firsthand?

Then you take that first step off the bus, plop your bags down, and realize within the first seven seconds a very unsettling truth: Hollywood is the most *un-Hollywood* place on earth. The shimmer and shine of Hollywood's beckoning lights are apparently only available when the cameras are rolling and the budget is set north of twenty-five million.

And yet as I chased my dreams, LA felt like the only sensible place to go.

It was Graduation Number Two. This time from a job, not a school. No one from my family flew in for the party this time. Probably because it was an office party consisting of badminton, laughs with coworkers I'll miss greatly, and mass quantities of what had been my favorite part about work — free food.

I wasn't leaving for a job; I was leaving for a dream and a girl.

The Real Deal?

Naomi and I had been dating for more than a year now, making the drive back and forth from LA to Santa Barbara on weekends. Or meeting halfway in a Denny's parking lot on a Tuesday night and getting home at 3:00 a.m. All reason and good sense would fly out of my Honda window the moment Naomi said, "I really want to see you."

And while Denny's parking lots are assuredly what eHarmony recommends for a proper date night out, it was time — to live in the same city, do the *"Meet the Family* Road Show," hang out on a daily basis, go grocery shopping, annoy each other with our secret quirks we both were sure we didn't have, and see if this thing was going to progress to a "dancing the 'YMCA' in a tux and wedding gown" kind of level.

Sure, we had our few explosions. Mainly due to my own insecurities detonating at inopportune times, hitting her with so much shrapnel that it put our relationship on life support.

Like the time I decided to pick a fight in the car, and all she could do was lie across the backseat of my Honda all the way home. Six hours away. Always a smart idea to provoke an epic fight fifteen minutes into a road trip back home.

A road trip with a significant other sounds like a romantic adventure when you're planning it at your kitchen table. But the moment that tire goes flat five hundred miles from home, it's every person for themselves.

I don't even remember what started the fight, other than my grand propensity to be stupid. But I do remember some of the choice words we had for each other in our pressure cooker on wheels. But isn't that how fights usually work? You rarely remember what you were fighting about, but you do remember what you yelled at each other while fighting.

Our relationship wasn't all romantic bliss, but it was real. I moved to LA to see if it was the *real-deal* real. I didn't want to see if I could live with Naomi for the rest of my life; I wanted to see if I could live without her.

Good-bye and Hello

As I filled every nook of my '93 Honda with my possessions, I was ready and excited to say good-bye to Santa Barbara. This was the place you lived *after* you really made it in LA, not before. I needed to go and do the work. It's a strange feeling when you can't wait to leave paradise.

Rob helped me pack up my things as we sorted through piles of clothes, receipts, and forgotten bananas that had gone unnoticed for years because we couldn't distinguish the difference between *that smell* and the natural aroma of five dudes in one house.

Our lives had become so intertwined it was hard to separate one from the other. Rob's stuff was mine and mine his, and the rest neither one of us wanted to claim. Or be the one to actually throw it away.

I left knowing Rob and I would always be close, but probably not in the same way as talking late into the night from top bunk to bottom. Unless my future wife was cool with taking Rob in as our roommate. I casually tossed the idea past Naomi a few times, and it never quite elicited an actual response.

Maybe that was more of a question if the ring ever actually got around her finger.

Mountain Mama

Naomi and I didn't feel moving in together was a smart choice, so I was dropping my things off at a 1930s bungalow in the town of Sierra Madre — a beautiful, funky city nestled up to the San Gabriel Mountains, only about a fifteen-minute drive from LA, *if there's no traffic*. Which of course there always is. But LA-ers love saying things like "if there's no traffic" as a proclamation that someday, I swear, no traffic will happen.

LA-ers are a surprisingly optimistic bunch.

I was moving in with four other roommates who were all acquaintances from college but who I had never really hung out with before. We were all converging on LA for different reasons, some for grad school, some just to live out a change and new adventure and thought Sierra Madre was the best place to make it happen. With a name like Mountain Mama, how could we not?

Sierra Madre is a mixture of the wealth of *The O.C.* with the hippieness of a '70s desert concert, *clothes optional*. As I moved my stuff into an upstairs bedroom that could be best described as "a large closet with a broken window and no insulation," I noticed instantly that our place had a slightly weird vibe to it. Everywhere there were fairy statues and hybrid-animal creations that looked like one of those pictures TV night-show hosts put together if two celebrities had babies.

Plus, there was a large steel box of bones chilling down in the basement, which a plumber stumbled across one day and quit the job right then and there.

The bungalow was a little light on the sexiness of LA but heavy on the terror. We could've rented it out to some Hollywood B horror movies and made a pretty penny.

Sitcomesque

This new bungalow, this new "home," was another reminder for me that life in your twenties will take you places you never knew existed yet at the same time were sure you'd never go.

Many of us envisioned the sexy, cool, sitcomesque twenty-something life where drinking coffee with unnaturally good-looking people and witty banter were our two mainstays. When instead we found ourselves back in our parents' house, sleeping under the same dinosaur bedspread or Tinkerbell poster. Or sleeping in a shoebox in the city with neighbors who fight loudly and then make up even more loudly. Or in my case now, a bungalow with a box of bones.

If someone was watching me, it might have looked like a sitcom. But it definitely didn't feel like one when I was actually living it out.

Jane with the Long T-Shirt On

No person better exemplified Sierra Madre's hippy ideals than our next-door neighbor, Jane — a former traveling hairdresser for Fleetwood Mac whose repeated claim to fame was that she possessed a lock of lead singer Stevie Nicks's hair. In a safe. In her house, which she was constantly inviting us inside to see. A request for which we quickly began running out of excuses to give for why it was not a "Stevie Nicks's dead hair" kind of day. The creepy woman mannequin that sat on her front porch and stared at my window all day was enough to tell me that if I went into her house, I was never coming out. Entering her front door would make the guy in *Misery* look like he was simply stuck at an awkward bar mitzvah.

Jane was somewhere between forty-five and sixty-five years old, with the voice of an eighty-seven-year-old man who put a sandpaper patch on the back of his throat. Since drugs were most definitely a mainstay of Jane's freewheeling, pocketing-hair days, it was hard to say exactly who Jane was, is, would be, or should be. On a bizarre daily basis.

With Jane, there was one thing you could always count on: When you parked your car in the back, she'd be out of her place before you exited your vehicle, wearing nothing but an oversized T-shirt (and I mean *nothing, zilch; please, God, don't let her pick something up today*), with a complaint about something new we were doing that was driving her crazy.

This from the lady who, like clockwork, at any time of the day or night, would scream at the top of her lungs at any neighborhood dog that had the audacity to raise its voice. And late at night, on separate occasions, she would put her hand through our back screen door, unlock it, come in, and turn off the dryer, if any roommate was foolish enough to run it past 10:00 p.m.

The fact she complained about us so much always felt a tad hypocritical.

Jane lived on the same property, so "next-door neighbor" might imply a little too much distance between us. Micah, who became my closest friend in the house, lived upstairs across from me in another sizeable closet. And when either of us sneezed, typically the first person to get there with a "bless you" was Jane. She was strangely polite about sneezes. Sometimes Jane would even stop us and reference something Micah and I had been talking about in our rooms the night before.

At least we got nightly entertainment from seeing what kind of outlandish new conversation we could make up to shock her.

If anyone taped any of those conversations, God help me.

Micah and I had both moved to LA with about the same amount of preplanning.

None whatsoever.

As our other roommates diligently worked their intense graduate programs or social work jobs, Micah and I were watching midday reruns of *MacGyver*.

I think we were both hoping our lives would turn out like one of MacGyver's inventions — the one part piece of wire, one part old helicopter engine, one part broken tennis racket used by a Soviet spy, who was surprisingly good at tennis, that MacGyver, under immense pressure, would tie all together with two seconds to spare, saving himself and a Vietnam village.

We were hoping we had the same sort of resourcefulness in us. But considering we were successfully getting ourselves dressed and ready for the day, half of the days, seeing MacGyver able to do so much with so little wasn't exactly the inspiration we needed. That and the fact that we were watching him at 2:30 p.m. on a Wednesday while licking the sleeve of our pepperoni Hot Pocket probably didn't help much either.

I went from sharing a room with Rob to living across the hall from Micah, and the two were actually really good friends. Honestly, they could've been brothers. If you ever met anyone who had something bad to say about Micah, you knew right away that person was a complete a-hole. He was full of grace, encouragement, strength, and good looks, with a smile that went from the top of one ear to the other. Plus, he was a man's man with the physique most men were secretly jealous of, though we'd never admit it. I might have had a bit of a man crush.

He could tie the knots you pretended you could, and after growing up as a missionary kid in faraway countries, Micah (I was pretty sure) could catch, kill, and clean a rabbit, all with his bare hands, if need be.

And if neither one of us could afford any more Hot Pockets, this was my fallback plan.

Micah had so much going for him, yet he couldn't quite get his life going. With his degree in biology, Micah was working as a part-time substitute teacher/part-time construction worker. He could've been the twentysomething poster child — lots of potential, with no path.

Yet he was still doing considerably better than I was. I wasn't working at all. Well, at least not in a job that actually paid something.

It wasn't like I didn't have *any* plan or purpose. In fact, I was now pursuing my dream of becoming a writer. No more cubicle. No more comfortable job. No more holding my dreams under water until they stopped squirming. I was a writer.

Before moving to LA, I'd been able to land a pretty well-known literary agent, which felt like the biggest win of my post-graduation life. Since you typically need a successful book to land an agent, but can't get a successful book without first having an agent, it felt like the catch – 22 I'd never be able to crack open. But with the introduction from a good friend who had already been published, I was able to send half of a manuscript to the agent, somehow trick the agent into thinking the manuscript had merit, and, before I had time to freak out, get me one of those agent-type people.

After years of ample twentysomething *unsuccess*, I felt like I possibly could be on my way to remembering that success did, in fact, exist.

Problem was — I needed a second half to my book. And I had no idea what that second half should be.

But I figured half the world goes to LA when they have no clue what they're writing, so I was sure the rest of my story was waiting to be discovered under the Hollywood sign or in the arms of Alec Baldwin. Or something like that.

I was a writer. I knew it. Problem was — no one had clued in the rest of the world.

CHAPTER TWELVE

MICAH, MACGYVER, AND ME

As I worked on my manuscript, I spent hours and hours at this big oak '70s table in the middle of our house. In between Jane shouting at Charlie (the dog next door) to shut up and music from Sufjan Stevens on repeat, calling my creativity to come out and play, I was very, very slowly crawling my way toward writing *The End*.

And when writing couldn't be harder, construction started directly next to us. And not someone just remodeling their living room. No, they were clearing trees, leveling ground, laying pipes and roads to construct a new twenty-five-house development nestled up in the San Gabriel Mountains directly next to us. Rumor was the city of Sierra Madre had been fighting against the development for years, and there was talk of "some happenings" to finally get it approved.

Perfect. There's no better way to discover and articulate life's answers than with a bulldozer digging fifteen feet from your head.

Micah would sometimes join me at the table on his computer, searching for a job that was him. Working as a part-time substitute teacher and construction guy, who just so happened to be working for a cross-dressing foreman (construction and cross-dressing may seem culturally contradictory, but when in LA . . .), Micah wasn't exactly on his life path. So he searched for it on Craigslist.

Free dirt, IKEA hand-me-downs, and a creepy date for

Friday night. Craigslist has these in spades. But your career? Well, there are almost too many amazing options to pick just one! Like choosing a box of cereal! Who wouldn't WANT TO MAKE SERIOUS $$$ IN YOUR FIRST WEEK!!??!?! With NO Expereance Necececessary!#%!! Just Bring Your Winning SMILE, urine sample, and $250 Startup Fee. THIS OPORTU-NITY WILLN'T LAST!@%%^$${!!!!}

For hours and days and months we assumed our positions — writing, job searching, Sufjan, Jane screaming, bulldozers doz-ing, Micah, MacGyver, and me.

As Micah and I sat and worked and struggled to move our lives forward, it felt like trying to pull a grand piano filled with one brick for every dollar we were still paying in loans for the college education that was supposed to accelerate us. And being that Micah was a missionary kid and I was a pastor's, this was a shiz-load of bricks.

Writing was now at a standstill. I was mostly trying to tell my own story, and yet my story didn't exactly feel like some-thing worth telling. I kept waiting for a mountaintop experience to describe, and then tell others how they could follow me to the top. But if they saw where my footsteps were leading now, I didn't think they'd exactly be rushing to follow.

With my savings account dwindling faster than my confi-dence, my plan to follow my dreams seemed like something I should've planned better.

Bankrupt

Lack of planning was a theme all around, as even the new development construction happening right next to us abruptly stopped one day, huge bulldozers sitting stoically in the expansive open space like modern twenty-first-century statues. There were huge pipes, roads, concrete foundations, but the new home development was lacking one little thing — *houses*. Apparently the budget had gotten out of hand, and the realities of the "Great Recession" claimed another victim. The company that had spent years trying to build didn't have much money left to do so.

Work and money were drying up for Micah as well. But he now had his first structured plan — to participate in a study for an experimental drug for serious depression that he'd seen an ad for on Craigslist.

The downsides: staying by yourself in a room for two weeks at a clinic and possible side effects, which included extreme paranoia; unquenchable thirst; extreme growth of male breasts; extreme shrinking of male testicles; manic, suicidal thoughts; and abnormally hairy shoulders. All that, and the ad was on Craigslist too.

The upside: the experimenters were paying $7,500!

As Micah presented his case why we both should do the study, if it hadn't been for the possibility of hairy shoulders, I would've said yes. Well, that and the possible reduction of my maleness. The thought of looking like Teen Wolf with tiny testicles didn't quite feel worth $7,500.

Ten thousand, however, would've been a different story.

Micah decided against participating in the study, mainly due to the desperate pleas from the other roommates, which actually ended up reducing him to a much more degrading way to make money — doing odd jobs for Jane.

As I sat at the table, agonizingly trying to put down one word after another, I'd look up to see Micah painting Jane's fence while she sat in her lawn chair directly next to him with a glass of lemonade, nothing between him and *all of her* but a long, white Grateful Dead T-shirt.

I was pretty sure we'd both have to look up to spot rock bottom.

And of course, this is when our university's alumni magazine arrived. Its mission: to expand our insecurities to unsafe levels until they were bound to explode.

Since all five roommates graduated from the same school, the alumni magazine would descend on us like a plague of locusts. The shining faces, the featured articles of people's amazingness, students we studied next to (who we were pretty confident would be working for us in the janitorial department) now being featured as the poster children of graduate success.

People starting nonprofits, making millions, or making babies.

While we had MacGyver.

Social media was bad enough, seeing everyone's Like-worthy lives unfolding before our eyes. But now it was as though our school was confirming what we already knew — our lives were not very Like-able. "Unemployed, unpublished author and part-time substitute teacher doing odd jobs for the craziest cat this side of the '70s" didn't exactly exemplify the outcome we'd spent a small fortune to see happen.

Nothing could make our lives feel more unglamorous than staring at the showcased glamor of others. I wanted to be the feature story, when all I had was an unfinished rough draft that no one knew or cared I was writing.

Success looks so sexy, until you're slushing through the muck and mundane to make it happen.

The End

Then one day I wrote *The End*. The moment snuck up on me like falling asleep. I didn't know it was happening until it was over.

I finally had a complete manuscript to send to my agent. In no time it was going to be lying on the desk of one pleasantly surprised publisher after another who would be frantically trying to get in touch with my agent, whilst frantically having their assistant figure out how to correctly pronounce my last name.

Of this I knew, for the Bible told me it was true. Or at least so I'd interpreted a few verses to make a fairly compelling case.

But before sending the manuscript to publishers, my agents wanted to send it to a few test readers first to see what people in my target audience thought. It sounded like a smart idea, so I sat back and anxiously awaited responses I was sure were going to be raving.

As my fate rested in the hands of complete strangers who merely had to pass the strenuous test of being in their twenties and being able to read, Micah was also facing a big next step. With only so much fence he could paint for Jane, he finally was ready for an actual step toward a full-time job. He was applying to be a lifeguard. And no, not a lifeguard for the neighborhood pool, but one for the Pacific Ocean. Maybe you've heard of it.

I was completely for the idea. One, it was better than having someone experiment on him with experimental drugs. Two, it was a good fit for Micah's strengths and personality. Three, he was excited about it. Four, I'd maybe seen an episode or two of *Baywatch* and was excited about the possibility of visiting him on the job.

To be a lifeguard, Micah had to do an intense physical challenge, one even more difficult than a contestant pouring green goo on her mother's head as seen on *Double Dare*. The lifeguard test consisted of basically running a half marathon in sand up to his knees and then swimming to Hawaii and bringing back three pineapples. Or something just as insane. As I was working on marketing proposals I could send to publishers along with my highly crafted manuscript, Micah was swimming for a month straight to prepare.

No more beer. No more *MacGyver*. Things were happening. There was forward movement.

Eat that, freaking alumni magazine.

D-Day

'Twas the day of days. We were invading our futures.

Micah left for his battle against the Pacific, and as I sat down in front of my computer, *there it was!* The email. The target readers had spoken, and as I prepared to look at their reviews, my heart raced as if I were actually stepping out of a boat on Normandy.

I opened the document of the readers' responses, and my heart soared as I read wonderful compliments on page 1. I'd dodged the bullet, and now I was safe. I thanked God.

Well, until I scrolled to page 2.

And a few things instantly struck me like an errant golf ball shot to my head:

1. The font had gotten noticeably smaller. *Strange.*

2. The title at the top of the page was "Things to Work On."

3. The page was lined with bullet points, each one piercing my skin, finding me in the hiding place where I thought I was safe.

I went on to read ten pages, in *10-point font*, of everything these mystery readers didn't like about the book — my voice, my story, my mom, and what I was wearing while I wrote it. If my agents hadn't dropped the font size, the destructive constructive criticism would've been longer than the manuscript itself.

The Un-Tipped Tipping Point

Naomi took me out to dinner that night, and a good thing she did because I couldn't have afforded it otherwise. As I shared the readers' responses, she did her best to cheer me up. She encouraged me and said this was my opportunity to make the book even better. But I could see in her eyes that even her half-full glass was dangerously close to falling off the table.

Dating an unemployed writer was bad enough; dating a writer who can't get his own agent to send out anything he's written makes things a little *too* real. Thank God that's half of LA.

I felt like I had spent my entire twenties waiting for my tipping point to finally tip. When it kept bouncing back and smacking me in my face and saying, "Better luck next time, buckaroo."

Freaking condescending tipping point.

Honestly, I wasn't sure there was going to be a next time. Fifteen different strangers had told me my baby was ugly. And even if that did happen to be the case, it wasn't exactly something that was quickly rectifiable.

As dinner progressed, Naomi told me about her day at work, which of course had gone really well. And of course I was really happy for her, well, that is, if it wasn't for the fifteen strangers I was envisioning watching me eat, critiquing the way I was holding my fork and sitting in my chair, while heckling me with "For a chubby guy, you sure don't eat much."

Naomi had recently made a big leap herself, switching careers from admissions counselor for a university to financial adviser for a bank. A natural career progression for someone with no business background. But of course after only six months working there, she was already doing really well.

Naomi possessed something in droves that was anemic in me — courage. And the ability to say, "I don't really care what others think, say, or feel I should do. This is the path I know I need to walk down. So just try to stop me."

Naomi had chutzpah. And I loved her for it. Actually I kind of just loved her. Period.

I fully realized it a few weeks before as we were driving in her two-door Mazda Miata, a car that made a coffin look roomy. I remembered looking at her and simply thinking, *I could drive anywhere with her and be at home. Even in this death trap on wheels.*

But how could I even think about broaching the big *E* word to see if she would agree to the big *M* word when I felt like such a big *L* word.

She was becoming a thriving businesswoman, and I was on the fast track to having people discover my writing 150 years after I was dead. And still hating it.

I wouldn't marry me. How could I ask her to?

You're Going the Wrong Way

Naomi dropped me off back home, and as I slowly walked up the steep steps to our bungalow, I saw Micah's Buick. He was back from his lifeguard audition. *God, I hope he made it to the next round.*

I opened the door and saw him lying on the couch, beer in

hand, staring at a black TV screen. I knew our D-Day wasn't a day of victory, but a day of disaster instead.

"What happened, Micah?" I asked as I sat down in an old wicker chair.

"I went the wrong way," he said simply.

"When driving to get there? Didn't you have directions?" I asked.

"No — in the ocean."

"In the ocean?" I wasn't getting it. Plus, my concentration was waning as the wicker dug into my back like I was sitting in a chair made from thick steel coils braided together.

"Yeah, in the ocean," he said taking a chug from his beer. "I was exhausted. Seventeen-year-old girls were passing me like they were on jet skis. And I missed the buoy I was supposed to turn at. By the time I realized it, I was so far off course I didn't have a chance."

"Wow. I'm sorry," I said, looking at the ground. "Really — seventeen-year-old girls? Passing you?"

"Yeah, man. Like aquatic animals. Those high school swimmers could've swum with one another on their backs and still lapped me."

I didn't know what to say, so I led with shared misery. "Well, I got the responses back from the target readers today, and they hated my book. I pretty much have to trash what I've been working on for the last six months and start over."

Micah sat there staring at his beer bottle, then back at the black screen of the TV. "Man, we don't have much to show for our time here, do we?" he said quietly, a question we both knew needed no answer.

The black television screen said it all.

I was thankful now for the wicker chair making large red

indentions on my back because at least it took my mind off things. Plus, if someone could actually sell a chair that felt like a torture chamber, then there had to be hope for us.

"Hey, guys, come up here!" shouted another roommate from upstairs, breaking apart the silence we couldn't have escaped by ourselves.

Micah and I went up into his room. "Out here. On the roof." We climbed out his window into the warm summer night. "Look. Over there."

We looked up into the black silhouette of the San Gabriel Mountains to see a bright orange light beyond the first mountaintop, growing with every passing minute.

"Oh my gosh, how far away do you think that fire is?" And as if on cue, we saw the first lick of fire climb over the mountainside as we heard a helicopter blazing across the sky. The fire must have still been miles away, but it was now heading downhill, and it looked like it was on a direct line toward us.

I'd never been up close to a wildfire before. That was all about to change.

The Fire

Evacuations started happening fairly quickly as neighbors began the process of deciding what part of their life deserved the cherished space in their SUVs. Evacuations were not yet mandatory, but if you did choose to leave, you couldn't come back. A few of our roommates quickly gathered things and took off as smoke began to fill the halls of our house. But Micah and I stayed. As insane as it sounds, this fire was easily the best thing we had going for us, and we were not going to let it out of our sight.

With the moon shining above, we climbed through a gap in the fence to the vast construction wasteland that was the new home development that never developed. We walked up a road to the highest slab of foundation at the top of the hill. They were assuredly planning the development's chef-d'oeuvres on this slab of concrete with the million-dollar view. That night, we got every penny's worth for free.

We sat in silence as we watched a raging fire grow so fast it was as if little terrorist squirrels were running around, dousing it with gasoline. You could feel its heat. You could hear the force of the wind it was creating, like multiple jets were taking off. Massive hundred-year-old trees exploded like they were ketchup packets put in a microwave. I looked at Micah, who used to be nothing but a black silhouette, and now I could see every detail of his face. The fire lit up our hiding spot like God was pointing a floodlight at us.

As we watched the awfully powerful, powerfully awful fire cascade toward us, all of my problems felt so insignificant. There was no room in my mind to think about wrong turns and negative reviews when we were staring down something that was consuming everything.

When your house is burning, you forget about the hurtful message on your answering machine.

We stayed up all night watching the fire's every move. If only MacGyver had been there. He could've put the whole thing out with nothing but a Super Soaker he scored from a local church's lost and found and a used ball of pink yarn — why yarn and why pink becoming hilariously clear as MacGyver escorted a family of deer over the last smoldering flame.

Unfortunately, MacGyver was unavailable, and as the fire drew closer and the blaring sirens of fire trucks intensified,

Micah and I quickly half snuck, half ran down the hillside. It seemed the inevitable course this fire was taking was about to become a 9-News reality.

The Town's Savior

The sun began to rise, the fire blending with the orange and pink of the new morning. The fire was only five hundred yards away now and on a straight line to our house and the city of Sierra Madre. As firefighters sped up and down the street, we stood on a corner across from our house with a small group of neighbors who had chosen not to evacuate. It was like we were the last people on earth. Some of these people had known each other their whole lives; some met on that corner that morning. Even crazy Jane was there, the quietest I'd ever heard her.

Standing there with the others as the fire neared, I strangely felt peace. We were all in this together. Destruction was coming toward us, but somehow I knew we were all going to be all right. We were connected by only one thing — a desire not to see the fire destroy the houses in front of us. And just the power of our collective presence made it feel that somehow we were going to prevail.

With the fire coming within twenty feet of our little bungalow, it was extinguished. Not one home damaged. We cheered together and high-fived, and I even found myself in a Jane embrace — who was, thankfully, wearing jeans on this special occasion.

And although firefighters had been heroically fighting the fire since the moment it started, it wasn't one last stand that put it out; it was something much more powerful. The vast empty space where homes or trees should've been standing became the best firebreak imaginable. The development that never was, the one Sierra Madre had fought for years, was now the town's savior.

I laughed as I stared at the last sizzled bush that the fire could get its fingers on. The town had failed to get its way. The building company had gone bankrupt. And it was only because of so much failure that so much was saved. Everything that went wrong had been exactly right. No good sense or reasoning would've ever planned it that way, but it was the perfect plan after all.

Our lives can feel the same way. It doesn't exactly feel like a good thing when you're sitting there watching your plans go up in flames like a brush fire. But let's be honest; we never really had a plan in the first place. Or at least not a good one.

We had a dream of making a difference or at least making braggable amounts of money, but we didn't have this strategic plan on how we were going to get there.

Amazing was just going to happen.

But maybe our twenties are not about things going as we planned, but about how we adapt, change, and grow when they don't.

Our twenties are about failing, tweaking, then trying again. They're about building a plan based on who you are, who you're not, and who you're becoming.

And somehow the failure that felt like the sixth-grade bully who used to sit on your head becomes your trusted business partner.

Regrowth

Later that day, neither Micah nor I was thinking about the alumni magazine. We were now television stars! Well, at least for our standard fifteen minutes. News stations ventured up to where the fire stopped, and we were there to gladly tell them all about it. First, the LA stations. Then Telemundo. And then a Japanese station. We were now worldwide. The media wanted to hear our story of valor and courage, how we were protecting our house from the ravenous flames. We didn't bother to tell them that, really, we just had nowhere else to go. And that we were just renting.

As life casually eased back into normal that day, Micah received a call. It was the lifeguard supervisor. They prefaced the call by saying "we really never do this," but they liked him so much they wanted to give him a second chance to try out to be a lifeguard.

Apparently they had seen *it* in him. They saw what I had seen every day from the kitchen window as he faithfully painted the fence of a crazy woman who was clothed in nothing but a T-shirt. They saw the potential and wanted to help him find the path.

Micah would go on to pass the test the second time.

And three years later, a crowd of people stood at the edge of the Pacific watching two eighteen-year-olds stuck in the middle of a fierce rip current and trying to stay above water. Six people called 911. One guy had time to pull out a video camera. No one jumped into the water to help.

Micah wasn't even supposed to work that day, but he had been asked if he could pick up a shift. He had finished that shift and should've left for the day thirty minutes earlier, but coworkers needed help with a project and he stayed to pitch in.

And then, sitting in his car, key in the ignition, he heard the 911 call.

He sprinted back to the beach, busted through the crowd of onlookers, and dove into the cold water of the Pacific. The young man was nowhere to be seen, and his companion, the young woman, was still visible as Micah swam toward her, but while he was still twenty yards away, he saw her become submerged under water. I would later hear from lifeguards that when someone goes under in the ocean, the chances of survival are small and become less likely with every second.

Micah reached the spot where he had last seen her. He began to dive and then come up for air — again and again. I don't know how many attempts he made. I don't know what thoughts raced through his head as his hands searched for life. I wonder if thoughts of how he had gotten to that day flashed through his mind, of how many failed plans and false starts led him to that place.

Micah dove down one last time, and within the small miracle of two hands touching, his hands found another.

Micah strapped a lifeless young woman onto a flotation device and began doing mouth-to-mouth resuscitation. Other lifeguards were reaching the scene, and they helped bring her in to shore. Micah stayed in the freezing water, diving repeatedly in a vain attempt to find the young man. This time, no miracle would touch his hands.

The young woman was admitted to the critical care unit, and many on the medical team wondered if her brain had suffered too much to recover. But months later, another miracle — Micah found himself talking with her at her bedside as she continued on the way to a full recovery. News stations wanted to interview him again — this time for real heroism.

Micah's boss, the man who had given him a second chance years before, described the video of Micah's rescue as "the most compelling piece of video I've ever seen in my thirty-four years as a lifeguard."

I think back to that old oak table and the image I saw through our kitchen window — Micah on his hands and knees diligently painting a fence as Crazy Jane, drink in hand, pointed out every spot he had missed.

Yet I missed something every time I had looked before. When I imagine that same scene now, I can see the Master standing there all along, diligently training his star pupil. In what it means to persevere. To cling to hope. To do good work, even when the work feels anything but.

When it seemed like Micah and I had failed in all our plans, The Plan put Micah exactly where he needed to be. Sometimes the best plans are the ones that don't go according to our plan whatsoever.

CHAPTER THIRTEEN

SHOPPING CART MAN

With hope and money dwindling fast, I took on the most terrifying part of writing a book — rewriting one.

I was learning the cold, meticulous reality of what it means to chase your dreams. You run after them full-out for months, and when you sit down to rest, you look over and see the same stuff you left at the starting line. Somehow you just ran in a very large circle, spending quite a bit of time and money to have the privilege to run it all over again.

The paradox of chasing your dreams is this: you start over — again and again — and yet somehow you're still making progress. You cling to hope.

It's not exactly "social media worthy," or something you'd brag about at the next party. But the cold hard failure of chasing your dreams is forging something inside you that you won't really see until you're humbled enough to know how to really look.

Progress is not displayed in what you've done but in what you know now not to do.

We Photoshop what it looks like to chase our dreams — when the real deal is an embarrassment that we'll never want to Instagram.

Fredinator123

With Micah now working every day, the house's blaring quiet filled my thoughts and ears. So Starbucks became the best LA office space $1.80 can buy.

I've now sat here in this coffee shop every day, searching for the guide to the rest of our lives. But as I wrestle with what is truth, my biggest concern will be whether I can get a table near an elusive outlet. My biggest complaint will be that they put too much ice in my iced vanilla coffee. One of my most pressing to-dos will be making a good playlist in iTunes to inspire me to write all those "answers."

But the world around me keeps interrupting. The ongoing traffic of coffee goers, the sea of laptops, and Lorde's CD on sale — the sixteen-year-old from New Zealand who's accomplished more than me with one line of song — all draw my attention to a different place.

So does the man who stumbles in every day with his own plastic cup. He goes straight to the milk, pours himself a cup of half-and-half, and downs it as quickly as possible before anybody can run him off.

Then there's the sixty-year-old man with a shopping cart, who every day makes the exact same rounds, in the exact same clothes, with earphones on — probably playing a "playlist" that's a little different than mine. He walks through downtown, checking newspaper stands for quarters. Every day.

Meanwhile, the Half-Caf-No-Foam Latte sitting next to me is clearly agitated because some stranger asked to share his table. He cannot be bothered. He has an online video game to attend to.

Such stark contrasts in the realities of our existence. Half-and-Half Snatcher. Shopping Cart Man. No-Foam Vigilante Video Gamer. Then there's me.

I'm broke. Let me just come out and say that, so it's not awkward later when I have to sell my computer on eBay and Fredinator123 from Des Moines ends up posting all of this on the Internet for me.

Chasing a dream is not very lucrative when it hasn't extended any farther than your own computer screen.

I have enough money left for one more month's rent, plus a dwindling $100 coffee/writing fund that my amazing former boss gave me in fives and one ten — a cash gift I haven't classified as "my money," making it much easier to spend on coffee every day.

Unfortunately today, the well of fives has run dry. My hand dipped in one last time, and my fingernails scraped along the bottom. All I pulled up was the lone ten-dollar bill. This piece of cherished paper I'd been gleefully hoarding. Saving the best for last.

But as I watched Shopping Cart Man make his daily rounds today, like he's done so many times before, I couldn't shake this insane thought: *You need to give Shopping Cart Man that ten-dollar bill.*

I tried to drown out this thought with gulps of coffee and loud music, but I could still hear its roar.

"But I'm broke too," I reasoned with myself. "In a month that could be me riding in that man's shopping cart. Or him in mine. Or switching off, as I'm sure we would work out some sort of pushing rotation."

I don't care. You need to give Shopping Cart Man that ten-dollar bill.

"No ... no ... you don't understand. This is my last ten — "

You need to give Shopping Cart Man that ten-dollar bill.

"Shut up ... no ... you don't get it."

No, you don't *get it. You need to give Shopping Cart Man that ten-dollar bill.*

"Fine!" I yelled out, coffee leaping over the edges of my mug. "Get off my back." Vigilante Video Gamer glanced at me as I finally succeeded in getting him to move to a different table. "I'll give my last ten to Shopping Cart Man. But promise me that if I do, you'll help me write a couple of really insightful pages."

I don't know if it's possible to bribe a conscience, but since it had compelled me to give away my last ten dollars I thought it was worth a shot.

I wanted to be a completely joyful, no-strings-attached giver. But all the caffeine had me on edge. That, and I'm selfish.

Out There

I walked outside and was instantly overwhelmed by the hot, smug LA air that feels like trying to cuddle with an exhaust pipe. I saw Shopping Cart Man sitting there, looking really tired, head in his hands, eyes closed. Sheepishly I stepped closer, to about ten feet away from him, and stood there, trying my best to chicken out.

"Look, he's sleeping. I can't give it to him now."

Give him the money.

I took a couple of steps closer when I was pummeled with a mighty smell of homeless. A scent so strong it was creating a protective force field around him.

"I can't do this."

Keep walking.

Then his eyes popped open. Years on the street had probably trained him well. In an act of valiant reluctance, I walked those final paces and held out my ten dollars.

"Can I give you this?" I asked.

He nodded yes.

"Have a good day" was all I could add.

He nodded yes.

I scurried back inside my Southern California Starbucks. Back to my seat. Back to my laptop. Back to my life. That was it. I'd done my deed. Now I could get back to solving all my problems again.

"There, you happy?" I whispered. "You better hold up your end of the bargain."

After I'd given him the money, Shopping Cart Man was gone.

Ten minutes later, he was back. He sat outside the tinted window right next to me. We were like old friends having a drink together, with just a thin piece of glass to separate us. Me in air-conditioning. Him in hundred-degree heat. A thin piece of glass that could have been the Berlin Wall for all the separation it created.

As I watched Shopping Cart Man, I saw what my donation had bought him. A 64-ounce Pepsi, a burger, a big bag of Flamin' Hot Fritos corn chips, and two lottery tickets.

He scratched the tickets first, which greatly excited me, my writing now a distant second. I envisioned him jumping up and dancing as the new million-dollar winner. I would run outside and grab his hands, and we would jump up and down in a circle. Laughing like sisters opening up our Christmas presents. We'd be the lead story on the eleven o'clock news, both of us standing by his shopping cart, arms around each other's shoulders like father and son.

The homeless man who finally caught his break. The young guy who valiantly (I'd leave out *reluctantly*) made it happen. We were going to be local legends.

But he quickly threw the tickets on the sidewalk, crushing our eleven o'clock debut.

He pounded down the burger and fries, and then he just sat back with his bag of chips. Slowly, meticulously, he took one bite after another and then threw the next chip to the pigeons around him.

Then something happened. It wasn't dramatic. If anyone else had been watching, they probably wouldn't have noticed or cared. But I'd been watching Shopping Cart Man almost every day for a month as he walked up and down the sidewalks. That day, as he sat there feeding the pigeons, he did something I'd never seen him do before.

He smiled.

He was feeding the pigeons around him. He was full, and he was happy.

His smile became my answer. A smile from feeding those who needed it more than him. It was a painting of profound simplicity. There was nothing more satisfying than to see him satisfied.

So yes, here in this coffee shop I sit, overwhelmed with it all. The luxuries, the laptops, and, most of all, the sheer number of options I have. Countless choices so abundant they jump in my bed at night like a litter of puppies, each one vying for my attention. And peeing on my bed.

I could do anything with my life. A fact that should excite me, but instead makes me feel like I drank two liters of coffee to wash down some Ritalin. Twitchy, anxious, and moving quickly in circles.

I don't think I've realized how rare it is to have choices. I've been so overwhelmed with asking, "What do I want to do with my life?" that I've forgotten what it looks like to actually live it.

In other cultures and at other times in our country's history, people didn't have options. At least not as prevalent or pronounced as we do today. My grandpa walked to his job at a paper mill for thirty years. Seven days a week. In Kansas rain, snow, or

Wizard of Oz-like winds. He worked not as a quest for significance, but to survive. He didn't ask if the job fit his strengths, passion, and values system. He worked to feed his family. He didn't check his gmail account while he was supposed to be on the line. No, he worked while he was working.

Our generation has more options at our disposal than any other in the history of humankind. We're told from day one that the world is ours. Instead of singing the ABCs in kindergarten, we chanted, "I can do anything; I can be anything."

But what happens when we feel like we're doing nothing? What happens when all the choices and options become the never-ending cereal aisle that we can never leave. What happens to us then?

When it seemed like I was doing nothing, I was stuck, disappointed, and hurt by my lack of talent and God's lack of faithfulness. Instead of moving forward, I did what I know how to do best: Complain. Moan. Punch my pillow and pout.

But why? As I sit here watching Shopping Cart Man smile, my complaining doesn't make sense. With every Flamin' Hot Frito he tosses to the birds encircling him, I feel something inside me begging to switch.

"*Enough!* Enough bitching and moaning. Enough adding to the world's suffering instead of trying to ease it. If you're overwhelmed with asking what you want to do with your life, remember that it's a gift to even have the time and space to ask."

What if I walked around actually believing I have a specific purpose for my life — to bring life to the world around me in the everyday? I'm not just talking about joining in on the latest provocative social justice issue. Not that I shouldn't. Or that I shouldn't still desire to impact the world. But it must start simpler and more everyday than that. It's not just about social justice; it's about being just in my daily social sphere.

You don't join a cause; you live in one. Every day.

I can't help humanity if I've forgotten how to be human.

It doesn't have to be monumental to be worthy of my effort. It doesn't have to be labeled "big" to be worthy of my time. It doesn't have to be "social media worthy" for me to take a picture. Every single day I have the chance to forget about my "problems" and help the world with theirs.

Do I have the courage to be faithful in the small? If I do, will I have faith that "the big" will take care of itself?

As Shopping Cart Man got up to leave, one thing became certain to me: Sitting around trying to squeeze out profound answers from my own shallow posturing was not working. I needed to dip my bucket into a deep well of wisdom instead of just trying to digitally create the illusion of one. I needed to talk to the hard-earned, grizzled experience of someone like my grandpa, who knew the meaning of struggle and perseverance and hard work.

I walked out of Starbucks and began formulating an idea.

A few blocks down, I saw Shopping Cart Man waiting on the opposite side of the street for the same red light I was waiting for. He looked my way and gave me a slight wave. I felt like he was giving me permission.

I knew what I needed to do next: I was going to go to the end to find my beginning.

CHAPTER FOURTEEN

**NEAR-
LIFE
EXPERIENCE**

"*Y*ou're going to do what?" Naomi asked, flipping through a magazine without looking at any certain page, or at me.

I've had some crazy ideas before, but after sharing with her my latest and hopefully greatest, she must have been seriously questioning my judgment. And hers for dating me. And maybe thinking that her next action item was going to be creating a profile on eHarmony.

At a point in our relationship when I should've been thinking about the possibility of getting married and living together, I had very different plans, which included living with someone else.

Well, actually it was a plan to be living with about 125 different people.

"I want to live in a retirement home," I said, trying to muster as much resolve and confidence as a person can have when uttering such a phrase while in his twenties. "I've been spending all these years trying to find the answers, talking with friends who know just as little as I do. I need real wisdom. I need to talk to people at the end of their story to find the truth for my beginning."

I eased back into the couch, clearly proud of my profound explanation. What else needed to be said?

"A retirement home? Really?" Naomi asked. Apparently I needed more.

"Yeah, think about it. Every neighborhood has one. This is a place packed with experience that our culture does its best to avoid because it's not bold or beautiful. But what would I learn if

I lived there? What stories would I hear while playing bingo and watching *Wheel of Fortune*? I could just be there — surrounded by wisdom — and write."

"But, Paul, weren't you going to start looking for a job?" Naomi asked. A valid question, for sure. Thankfully I knew it was coming and had all the details worked out.

"Well, this will be even better than a job. Because I'll make the whole experience into a documentary film!"

I was on the fast track to wealth galore. Naomi could scratch eHarmony off her to-do list.

Near-Life Experience

Near-Life Experience. It was the perfect name for the film. I later had to speak to the lead singer of a death metal band by the same name to ask for permission to use it. But other than that, the name was flawless.

I had the name of the film.

Now I just needed a film. And there were just a few details I needed to work out.

1. How does one go about actually filming a documentary? I didn't even own a camera, let alone know how to use one.

2. How do I convince a retirement home that letting a twentysomething with no film experience into their home to film is a good idea? And, well, live there for free. I couldn't afford a room at the Motel 6, let alone a retirement home with all their fancy Jell-O desserts.

3. How do I figure out everything else? Like most of my ideas, there were a lot of wrinkles, and I couldn't afford the iron to help smooth them out. But I was in LA. This is how 95 percent of everything gets made.

Or so I kept telling myself.

I didn't know what I didn't know, which is a powerful place to start. Or an extremely stupid one. Time would tell. But when you set yourself to pursue something *no matter what* and just take one step forward into the unknown, a way opens.

Or so I kept telling myself.

Hopefully I would actually be right this time.

168 Film Festival

I started mentioning my idea to a few very close friends (living in a retirement home wasn't exactly something I was bragging about at parties quite yet), and someone mentioned the 168 Film Festival in LA. It was a competition in which each competitor had a week to make a short film, and the best films would be up for awards and shown on-screen at the historic Alex Theater in Glendale, California.

On-screen? Historic? Only seven minutes long? Sign me up! I'd make a short film and then use that to help raise money for the full-length. That sounds like something a smart person would do.

I had the semblance of a plan. Now I needed people to help.

Stanley

The first and only person I could think of calling was my friend Stanley. He was one of the seven guys I lived with during my senior year of college. He also was currently living in LA and was the only person I knew pursuing a career in the film industry. Which meant he had a camera! And he was typically doing any odd job remotely related to film, free or paid. So I hoped

Stanley would be my guy and would be willing to work on the extreme free side of the spectrum.

Stanley grew up in a small mountain town in Colorado and was known on our baseball team for having actually worked on a railroad — therefore being tougher than the rest of us. He had the grip of a body builder, the beard of a mountain man, and the body flexibility of a piece of wood dipped in concrete. Stanley was also smarter than the rest of us, though he was much too humble, and smart, to ever make us realize it. Somehow he made me feel that my degree in communications studies was comparable to his in engineering.

One of the best things about Stanley is he has one of those "what laughs should sound like" kinds of laughs, full of actual, joyful laughter. And Stanley is the nicest guy you've ever met, who also happens to love listening to Tool and watching obscure horror movies.

Stanley was the real-deal kind of hipster who would've never been caught dead labeled as such. LA and he fit like a railroad tie and a repurposed coffee table.

I called Stanley and told him my documentary idea, and before I even got to the end of the story, he said he was in.

Every crazy dream needs an equally crazy partner. Or you're just crazy alone. And that's when people invite you to stay with the really friendly nurses in that building with no windows.

* * *

We heard that the 168 Film Festival was putting on a mixer where competitors could connect, share their ideas, and find help. Stanley was pretty far on the introvert scale, and I leaned that way too, so we would've both rather been put in a blender than attend a mixer. But with no clue where to go or what to do, Stanley and I went to mix or be mixed.

I don't know what we were hoping to find there. Maybe an extra cameraman or soundman. We didn't have a high entry bar. Just a pulse and price tag totaling zero. But as we embarked into the awkward world of networking and elevator pitches, it took only fifteen seconds of pitching myself before I was questioning my idea and my entire reason for being.

Who am I to try to pull off something like this? How can I try to convince someone to jump in an elevator with me when it's hanging by one sheared cord that would make even MacGyver feel slightly nervous?

Networking felt like being in high school again, trying to drum up the courage to ask a girl to prom. The little confidence I possessed leaked out of a small pinhole like a deflating balloon. The more I tried to blow, the more my hot air escaped.

After an excruciating hour, I found Stanley and was ready to ward off networking like dysentery.

"No, wait. You won't believe who I met," Stanley said as he turned toward the back of the room. I followed, astonished that Stanley had met someone and was excited about it. "There she is."

That night we didn't find a camera guy or sound guy. We found a Ruth.

The Book of Ruth

Ruth was in her late thirties or early forties, Filipino, a physical therapist with zero experience in film and more faith in God and joy for life than all of Rhode Island combined. (If the fine people of Rhode Island were to ever meet Ruth, I'm sure they would all agree.)

Stanley would later tell me the story of meeting Ruth in line.

As he shared our idea with her, Ruth began whispering, "Praise Jesus. Thank you, Jesus!" Then yelling, "Yes, Jesus. PRAISE YOU, FATHER!" Louder and louder she chanted as she grabbed Stanley the introvert's hands and jumped up and down.

"God told me to come here tonight," Ruth said, interrupting Stanley in midsentence. "He said someone needed my help. I had no idea why I was coming. Now I know God sent me here tonight for you."

I can only imagine what was going through Stanley's mind, with his engineering degree and analytical faith, as he was now in the grips of sheer shouting, jumping emotion. But as Ruth told her story, it turns out she and God did have something up their sleeve.

Ruth was a physical therapist who, crazily enough, specialized in working with the elderly and had a passion to give them a platform for telling their stories. She told us she traveled around to retirement homes and could get us into a few to film.

I couldn't believe it! We went to a film mixer, and there we found our in to retirement homes. Like searching for a missing hairbrush and finding your lost car keys instead.

When you walk forward, a way opens. The door you hoped would open usually slams in your face, while you're ushered in the door you actually needed to go through all along.

Let the Filming Begin

The first night we were scheduled to film, I drove the hour and a half to Rancho Cucamonga from LA, which was only supposed to be about a thirty-minute drive, *if there's no traffic.*

Stanley was the sound, lights, camera, *everything* guy. All I had to do was be on camera and ask questions. But as my insecurities wrapped themselves around my heart and threatened to hold it ransom, I felt like Stanley had the easier job.

Our first interviewee was Tom, a World War II vet who now spent most of his time in a wheelchair at his daughter's house. I sat in their dimly lit living room with nervous excitement channeling through my bones. I was going to get my first taste of whether this idea was going to work or fall flat. What wisdom would this man share with me and possibly the world?

Ruth stood next to Tom's sixteen-year-old grandson, trying unsuccessfully to make small talk, while Stanley busily set up the lights and microphones as I did my best to help without breaking anything. We couldn't afford much in the way of equipment, so we begged for and borrowed as much as we could. We weren't able to get a boom mic, the microphone you use to drop in directly above the shot, so Stanley had amazingly jerry-rigged a microphone onto the end of a light stand with duct tape. If anyone had the illusion we were pros, our boom mic would amplify a different message.

I sat down next to Tom and tried my best to make small talk to help him feel comfortable, but it didn't seem to be working. Tom looked anxious and confused, and I was beginning to wonder what Ruth had told him about what he was getting into. The lights switched on. I watched Tom's eyes grow large under that terrifyingly bright reality of "there's nowhere to hide."

"Okay, we're rolling," Stanley said.

I looked at Tom, all the questions I'd written down in front of me blurring together.

We sat and kind of just stared at each other like an awkward teenage couple, neither of us knowing who was supposed to make the first move.

Finally I blurted out, "What helped you through hard times?"

Tom looked at me. "Say what?"

"Was there anything that helped you through hard times?" I asked again a little louder.

Tom looked at me and stared.

"What helped you through hard times?" I asked again.

Tom sat there motionless and stared some more. It didn't seem like he was formulating an answer.

"Hard times. When you had hard times, what helped you through?" I asked again, even louder, with as much comforting sincerity as my voice could muster.

And I waited. And I waited. And waited, stuck in that silent space on camera that feels like it lasts a month, where the more you squirm the worse it gets.

Finally I could see Tom's eyes move and his body shift as it looked like an answer was about to spring forth. I leaned closer, anticipating the truth that was about to enlighten us all. It was finally happening. His lips moved, and he said, "Well . . . nothing much."

For the next hour I tried every question I could think of to pull from this man the truth that informed his life, that helped him survive World War II, but it was not meant to be. It was like trying to interview a Ukrainian who spoke no English and his translator was running late.

We thanked him for his time and quickly packed up our stuff. We drove to the next houses, and the two remaining interviews followed Tom's unfortunate lead.

As we drove back to Ruth's house, packed tightly into my Honda Civic hatchback, the shifting gears were the only noises breaking the deafening silence. If you had eyes and/or ears, you knew the first round of interviews weren't exactly going to win us an Academy Award, let alone get us into the film festival.

I felt like that button on a pair of pants that's dangerously holding on by a single thread. One wrong move could pop the whole thing off and leave me pantsless. And everyone pointing.

When you feel like most of your twenties have been a failure, any little piece of evidence that helps support that fact feels unbearable. Failure used to be my uninvited guest that broke into my house, ate my food, and used my bathroom, refusing to spray any air freshener before I could kick it out.

Now I was becoming used to it. I felt like I was going to bed and leaving the front door cracked, just to make it easier for failure to come in. Failure was quite at home in my house, and no matter how badly I wanted it to go, I felt powerless to do anything about it.

Then from the backseat, as if she was reading my thoughts, Ruth sat up and went directly to the heart of the silence.

"If we're faithful in our actions, we allow God to be faithful in the results. It's not our job to make this film happen; it's our job to just keep filming."

Then she sat back and was silent again. Neither Stanley nor I responded. There was no need. It looked like the process of making a film about finding life's answers was going to produce a few of its own.

I wanted to live life without everything having to be a lesson. I was beginning to realize that's not the way life works. Those who know the most know how much they have left to learn.

But dang, if just one freaking thing could work out like it was supposed to! I swear I'll volunteer to pass out the "Getting to Know You" cards at heaven's gate for my first 250 years.

The Retirement Home Luau

A few days later, we were back in the filming saddle. Ruth had somehow convinced a retirement home manager to let her come in with her entire family, throw a party in the lobby, and have Stanley and me film the whole thing. Ruth probably could've gotten us into the White House with an oversized, unmarked black bag if the film called for it. She wasn't exactly someone you could say no to. And even when you did, she had this magical ability of not really hearing you.

Stanley and I walked into the retirement home lobby, and as we turned the corner I wasn't sure what to expect. Ruth did not disappoint. A karaoke machine was set up in the middle of the room, with lyrics displaying on the big screen and Ruth singing "Shout to the Lord" into a microphone, wearing a hula skirt, bright pink shirt, and leaf halo around her head.

Real life is much more interesting than anything scripted.

The night was a blur of interviews. We were getting great bits of wisdom from all kinds of different residents as we bounced from one interview to another. The idea was coming to life in front of us.

My favorite interview was with two best buds, Candido and Fred. They were kind of like the retirement home's Bert and Ernie with a splash of Latino. (Ernie does have that orangish-brown going on, though. Maybe his parents were from Chile?)

When I asked Candido and Fred what I should do with my life, Fred told me a story about his foot doctor and how much money he makes for clipping his nails. He recommended I look into it.

Then Candido told me, "There's four careers I wish I could've done: a scientist, a lawyer, a specialist engineer, and the one who puts candy in the machine. You know the one who comes and gets the change — what are they called?"

"Umm ... guy who puts candy in the machine. I guess that's what you call him," I responded.

"He works a lot of hours, though," Fred chimed in.

"But that's what I'd be — the guy who puts candy in the machine. It's a good job, no?" Candido asked me.

"Yeah, and you get to eat a lot of candy!" I said, laughing.

"Yeah!" Candido responded with a smile and then quickly dropped his brow. "But I can't eat candy, though; I'm diabetic."

We were getting documentary gold.

The night ended with me holding a mic in front of a sea of elderly residents, singing a duet rendition of "Amazing Grace" with one of the white-haired women.

Life will take you to many unique and unusual places you never knew you'd visit, but places you'll now never forget. And later you'll look back, thankful that the detour you hated led to your favorite memory of the trip.

We left that night with hope. Maybe, just maybe, we might be able to pull this film off. We only had something like the *d-o* of a documentary and only had five days left to finish it. But when you somehow make a killer appetizer that actually looks like it did on TV, a whole seven-course meal suddenly feels possible.

Ethel and Roy

We saved the two best interviews for last. Ethel lived in a retirement home in Pasadena. Naomi had recently become her financial adviser and instantly fell in love with her. Roy lived at home with his wife, and he was my roommate Micah's grandfather.

Ethel grew up in London during World War II and had amazing stories about diving into stores as German bombs exploded overhead. She was full of joy and life, and at eighty-five years old, she still had dreams of publishing an inspirational book of quotes.

Roy wasn't far away from Ethel in the 1940s as he fought on the Pacific front for the United States during WWII — a scared teenager from the farm with a promising baseball career that would lead him after the war to a contract with the New York Yankees.

Both Ethel and Roy were brimming with life. Hearing the details of their stories, of the decisions and events that were strung together like fine pearls to create two successful lives, was beautiful. There wasn't an ounce of regret or remorse on their faces, but a complete peace, knowing they had run their races well and yet still hadn't stopped running.

Ethel told me the story of how she got married to her husband, Victor. Having moved to the United States after the war, she had been dating Victor, who was from Romania, for only a few weeks when he received the sudden news that he was going to be deported.

Ethel explained. "Really, the decision was simple. I told him that all we have to do is go down to the courthouse and in a few minutes we'll be married, it will be done, and we can work out the details afterward." They were married until he passed away just a few years back. "With marriage I think everyone is doubtful, but once you're married, then you start making your own personal history, and that joins you together."

We need a five-year engagement and a ~~$15,000~~ $25,000 wedding budget to make marriage happen; Ethel needed five minutes, and for Victor to put on a clean shirt.

Sitting on Roy's couch, we heard about how he traveled around as a baseball player with teammates who would later enter the history books as some of the greatest. And then one day, he just decided it was time to give up his dream.

"I had a young wife and baby at home, and I couldn't justify being away from home so long. So I quit, went into sales, and did that for the rest of my life ... A lot of people know how to make money. Very few people know how to live."

There was such a deep simplicity to both Ethel's and Roy's lives. They both possessed profound wisdom to make complicated things very uncomplicated. They hadn't lived their lives plagued with doubt or depressed that they might have chosen a wrong path. They chose a direction and just walked. Roy told us the secret of what kept him moving forward: "If God is for me, who can be against me?" I'd listened to this Bible verse countless times before, but this time, sitting in Roy's living room, I actually heard it.

My life has been strapped to a roller coaster, my emotions and my value peaking or bottoming out, depending on the details of that day. And how long I linger on the Internet. Browsing the Internet is like window-shopping to buy another life. Linger too long, and you'll leave with a pair of shoes you can't afford.

I'm constantly analyzing the trajectory of my life, like an intense NASA engineer, instead of just enjoying the view up in the air. Ethel and Roy lived with a faithful, steady consistency.

I am continually plagued with doubts and fears that I'm making the wrong choices, and then I use the Internet for confirmation. And that the spot on my arm is, in fact, cancerous. I mean, look at the pictures; it's a spitting image! Ethel and Roy simply walked forward, knowing it all was going to be fine.

I walk forward and then freeze, like a frightened horse waiting for something to jump out and attack from behind the next bend.

As Ethel said to me right before our interview ended, "I found in my life that circumstances change. They don't stay the same way forever; they change a lot. There will be things we enjoy very much, but there will also be things we don't enjoy. So just concentrate on the things that are good and make the most of them, because when you move on and it changes, they will be gone. And ignore the things you don't like because they will be gone too."

The final scene we wanted to film for the documentary was Roy and I walking together to a little green patch behind his house, where I got to play catch with a former Yankee. Even in his eighties, Roy could throw a strike. As we tossed the baseball back and forth, I found myself laughing more than I had in a long time.

It was a laughter free from anxiety. I'd lived so joy-less for the last few years as I searched for the right conditions to be joy-full again.

I'm realizing that conditions don't dictate joy; a healthy mind and heart do.

As Roy said to me that day we played catch, "You know, it's the simple things in life that are the most profound. Sometimes it takes us a long time to realize that."

The Film Festival!

Stanley stayed up for two days straight editing our film to get it done in time. And for his amazing work I tripled his pay. Nay, quadrupled it! With one hour to go before the deadline, I rushed over to the 168 Film Festival with a DVD titled *Near-Life Experience*.

We had done it. We had created something. I drove home not caring at all if they chose our film to be featured or nominated for any awards. The outcome wasn't really important to me anymore. We had finished the process. That was all I needed.

A few weeks later, Stanley called. "Paul, have you looked at their website?"

"Whose website?" I asked, trying to pry away my attention from my writing.

"The film festival."

"No, why?"

"Go there. Right now."

"All right, hold on. Going there ... okay, I'm there."

"Scroll down."

"All right, scrolling, scrolling ... *wait*, what? We're up for best documentary?"

"Yeah, man! And there's only one other film nominated in our category!" Stanley shouted.

"Wait, *our* film? Up for best documentary?"

"Well, unless it's a typo or there's another *Near-Life Experience*, but yeah, looks so!"

"Wow. *Our film?* Wow! Our film! Hold on, I have to call Naomi!"

Up On the Big Screen

The theater was packed the night of the festival. We watched film after film as time moved agonizingly slow, like the final afternoon before summer break. We sat next to our friends and significant others, and as our movie began its debut, I'm pretty sure both our hands were gripping the armrests as if we were women delivering babies — butt first.

Sitting in a theater seat as one's face is projected in all its twenty-foot pixelated glory is a nerve-racking feeling.

How is the audience going to respond?

How did I get so fat?

How can I somehow still look unattractive standing next to an eighty-three-year-old with a hump?

As the opening credits rolled, I thought of the last time my work went out to the world — and mystery readers ripped it to shreds. If I was about to painfully witness the same thing, real time, by a few hundred people, my next move was going to be to Siberia to harvest rocks.

But then a glorious thing happened. The audience laughed. And then howled at Candido and Fred talking about foot doctors and wanting to put candy in the machine. I leaned deeper into my seat and let the laughter of the audience wash over me. The final scene of Roy and me playing catch went dim as the audience clapped and cheered. I could've died right then and taken my post handing out the welcome packets at the pearly gates.

We didn't end up winning Best Documentary that night. The other film was a Holocaust documentary. Don't ever step into the ring against a Holocaust documentary. Picking our film to win would've been like picking *Air Bud* over *Schindler's List*. Stanley's and my acceptance speeches would have to wait for another time. Yet we didn't need an award to feel like we had won.

Near-Life Experience Continued

For the next few months, living on very little, I pursued having a near-life experience to the fullest.

I'd never really considered myself a "creative person." Creating terrified me. It made me feel insecure compared to all who have actually done great works. But I was learning that creating made me feel alive. I was beginning to understand that no matter what job I did, I always needed to be creating something or I was going to slowly cave in.

A taste of sweet, tangible success after years of bland and bitter was giving me the courage to go out, look stupid if need be, and try for the big.

I was cold-calling prominent USC film professors and getting them to agree to meet me for coffee. I got a proposal accepted by the International Documentary Association so the film could receive tax-deductible donations. I signed up a talented cinematographer to take a low fee and agree to live with me for a month in a retirement home. And then the biggest win of all — after meeting with the director and the board, I got a retirement home to agree to let me come in, film, and live there for free! And eat all the fancy Jell-O I wanted!

The retirement home was located in Santa Barbara, California, just next to the University of California Santa Barbara on Illa Vista Street, which is known for being one of the biggest party streets in California. The juxtaposition of frat parties next to bingo night was the perfect setting for the story I wanted to tell.

Then I got my first donor for the film. And another. I had meetings with other organizations that were interested in giving more. A crazy idea was transforming from a dream into something that had real potential. Now my to-do lists were energizing, not overwhelming. Nos and setbacks that would've crushed me before did little to faze me. I was combining something I was passionate about, something I knew was important, with a skill set I was growing into.

I was learning that passion + values + skill is a powerful place to operate from.

I couldn't take the next steps fast enough. Well, until I got a voice mail.

The Call

I woke up to find a message in my voice mail box from a film director I'd met with a few weeks back. All he said was, "Hey, Paul, call me." Which meant either the news was too good to leave in a message, or too bad. I was hoping for the former. Unfortunately, my hope was deferred.

He told me he found out that HBO had just released a documentary film. About a twentysomething guy. Living in a retirement home for a month. To find life's answers. And the guy even looked like me! It was like I was trying to create an identical replica of his film to pass off as my own.

I sat on the front porch couch at our Sierra Madre bungalow and didn't move for hours. I couldn't believe all the amazing, timely open doors that had led me this far. And now an equally amazing closed door slammed right in my face.

I could've tried to twist the premise of the film to make it feel different. Maybe brought in a pet ferret to live with me or challenged the elderly to compete against me in some physical challenges, but it just didn't seem right. It felt over. I had walked down this path longer than most, but it looked like the result was going to be the same. Another dead end. Another failure.

But as I sat on our front porch couch, which smelled like wet leaves frosted with black mold, this failure felt different. It felt like a good kind of failure, that of having truly gone for something 100 percent and having it just not work out. I experienced a lot of small successes embedded into a failed end result.

This failure was something I could build on, even if what I was building had completely fallen apart.

Ever since college, I've wanted to become an overnight success, which basically means I wanted to do one thing fairly well with a marginal amount of work and become insta-mazing. And then ride that wave for five years until I could be cast on *The Real World C-List Celebrity Apprentice Survivors of New York*.

However, I'm learning that overnight success is a seductive lie. Success doesn't happen in a night; it happens in the thousand nights that no one will ever write a song about.

There are overnight sensations, to be sure. Take a crazy fall off a ledge while crushing grapes or have someone Auto-Tune your interview, and millions of people might come across you. An overnight phenomenon is an everyday thing now in the Land of Internet.

However, just as a lottery winner often ends up bankrupt in less than a year, an overnight sensation can go up quick and then fall back down at the same speed because there is no platform to support it. An overnight sensation is like a shooting star — a brief blaze that quickly burns out.

The moment I'll truly be ready for success is the exact moment I stop obsessing over being successful.

A true overnight success is someone who has carried bucket after bucket of water to fill up a well. People celebrate you the moment it all spills over, without realizing the ten thousand buckets you carried to make it happen.

It was time to start over. Again. And the decision I would make next would forever change my life.

CHAPTER FIFTEEN

"Do you see that?" I asked Naomi as I pointed at a red tin box floating toward us in the icy waters of a Rocky Mountain river. "Is that a box? What in the world?"

"Yeah, I think it's a box... Hey, let's go back to the car," Naomi said, apparently not quite as intrigued about this mystery box as I was.

"I have to see what that is." Before Naomi could begin to protest, I was off and running down the bridge we'd been standing on.

"Who cares about that box? Come back." Naomi yelled over the strong wind cascading down the valley. "Let's go back to the car. I'm freezing!"

My pulse was racing faster than my legs as I hurried off the bridge to try to fish this box out of a mountain stream in Colorado. I *had* to get it. I mean, how many times do you see a red tin box floating down a river in the middle of nowhere? What was inside?

Gold?

An old Mickey Mantle baseball card?

An "I need help" message from a trapped miner who had been pinned down by a boulder and had been surviving on stream water and bugs for the last thirty years?

The possibilities were endless.

I ran through snow up to my knees like a kid in a snowball fight and grabbed a long stick to try to fish the box out of the stream. But the wind was determined to keep the box in the water and kept pushing it away from me. As I saw the tin box escape down the rapidly moving water, there was no time to think. Good thing I'd become quite proficient at doing just that! I stepped on one rock in the river and then another, until there were no more rocks. Then I just stepped in.

"Have you lost your mind?" Naomi yelled from the bridge, but her voice and needless wisdom sounded miles away. I didn't even feel the ice water filling my socks. All my attention was focused on rescuing the box. And with two more quick steps I reached out and slipped my fingers around the corner of the ice-cold tin. I had it! My heart soared. Then it hit me that freezing mountain water was filling my shoes, and I could no longer feel my face or fingers. But I had the box!

I ran back onto the bridge, holding the prize that might have just given me pneumonia. Naomi stared at me, her eyes saying more than her mouth ever could.

"Listen, something's in there," I said shaking the box. "Here, I'll let you open it." I handed the box to Naomi as if I were letting her open the last piece of chocolate on earth.

Naomi sighed and slowly grabbed the box, most likely while having an internal dialogue with God about how it was possible she had gotten so far out of his will to be on this bridge with me.

As she lifted the lid, I studied her face, which looked like she was trying to decipher an optical illusion. Her hand reached into the red tin box and pulled out a smaller, black velvet box that could only be interpreted as housing a ring.

If you didn't already see it coming, the red tin box floating down the river was a setup. And the only reason I waded through the icy-cold Rocky Mountain stream to grab it was that it held my wedding ring! As Naomi looked up, holding the black velvet box, I was down on one knee in the snow. (My pant legs were already frozen solid, so at least it provided a force field from the snow.)

There may not be a more terrifying moment in a man's life than when he's down on one knee. His future hangs there in proposal limbo as he waits for a thumbs-up or thumbs-down. The words that come out of his mouth are a complete haze.

Men are taught to be strong, brave, and always in control. Then you find yourself holding up a tiny little ring, like a five-year-old who found a prize in his cereal, asking a girl to take it and hold on to it forever.

On the one hand, you hold that ring, overcome with terror that you've greatly misread all the signs that led you to thinking this was a good idea. And it's going to be a long, long drive down the mountain.

On the other hand, you're also secretly slightly terrified that if she says yes, you're going to have to pretend like you know what to do next! When it took all your mental fortitude just to make it to "will you marry me?"

I have no idea what came out of my mouth on the bridge that day, but I sure can remember what came out of hers. And as I burst up like a rocket that had been waiting to be launched into orbit, I was hoping her decision to join me on this journey wasn't going to end in a crash landing.

Young Adultish

Although I hadn't yet crossed the line into adulthood, I could at least spot it on the map.

I was getting married now, for grown-up's sake.

Sure, I didn't exactly have a job, as I was still an aspiring filmmaker and aspiring author — my book now in the editing of my edits from my previous editing phase. So with a ring now snug on Naomi's finger, it was beginning to fully dawn on me that I needed a real job again. "Aspiring" doesn't exactly pay the bills.

With my $1.80 rent at Starbucks now putting me in debt by $1.75, we sat across from smiling wedding photographers as I'd think, *Wait a second, Mr. Photographer; you're charging how much for a couple of hours' work? Oh, your wife is photographing with you. How cute. However, you do realize we're not asking you to do brain surgery on any of the guests, right? Just click a button while they're smiling.*

I had sold all the stock I owned from my short season of sound fiscal planning to buy Naomi's ring. Now the only items I was plopping down on the marriage table were a potato sack full of college debt and loads of aspiring potential.

At least I could go to sleep at night peacefully, knowing Naomi wasn't in this for the money. Not sure, though, if she could do the same . . .

Job Hunt Part Deux

It became the "staying alive, searching for a job" reality once again.

I applied and interviewed for all kinds of jobs around LA, looking for that dream job that was *me*. I tossed out job applications like candy in a crowd of five-year-olds whose parents, unfortunately, taught them way too well not to take candy from strangers. Usually my job search would end with me sitting on the ground, eating all the candy myself.

I was applying for jobs smack-dab in the middle of the Great Recession of the twenty-first century — "hiring freeze" my greatest nemesis. As jobs were being cut faster than prices at a Walmart clearance sale, finding that dream job (or any job, for that matter) was unfortunately a battle I was still clearly not winning.

Long String of Nos

The job I was most excited about was being a worldwide travel guide for Disney Resorts. The requirements said I needed to be at least bilingual — preferably trilingual or quadlingual — and have extensive world-traveling experience.

Well, I took two years of high school Spanish and could successfully recall my name was Pablo. And my world travel hadn't exactly gone across any oceans. But job requirements are more soft guidelines than rigid musts, right? So I applied. I'm still waiting for that call back. Maybe my travel experience — numerous trips to Hutchinson, Kansas, to see my grandpa — didn't fit their soft guidelines. Apparently they'd never experienced the wondrous world that is Kansas.

That's their problem, not mine.

As things became increasingly desperate, I interviewed at a telemarketing company to sell extended car warranties. Yes, a telemarketing company. I thought the interview went well, and as I walked out of their office, I couldn't believe I was actually excited about the possibility of working as a telemarketer.

They told me to call the next day to see if I got the job. I did. No one answered. I left a message. I waited two days and then called again. No answer. I left a message. For a week I did this.

I couldn't even get a telemarketing company to call me back. If irony paid, I would've been loaded.

My favorite interview was for a company that sold meat door-to-door. Steak, chicken, pork. In a truck all day around Los

Angeles driving a freezer truck as a meat pusher. I liked meat. I could get excited about meat. I figured I could sell meat. Why not drive a meat truck?

It would be like driving the adult ice cream truck. I would blare some Springsteen "Born in the USA" from my speaker and watch businessmen burst out of the door, jumping up and down with cell phones in hand, pleading with their wives for an advance on their allowance.

It would be magical.

I got up at 6:00 a.m. to go on a ride with one of their current employees. Her name was Darlene. She wore a beige sports coat, beige culottes, a bright blue bandana, and layers of blood-red lipstick. She liked selling meat. More importantly, she liked selling God. At one point she was giving me her Jehovah's Witnesses business card and telling me to visit her and her family someday.

By the end of the day, after going door-to-door in Hollywood pimping pork chops, the lure of "traveling meat salesman" had worn off. Plus, how could I sell meat with my new business idea — religious business cards.

"Here, let me give you my card."

PAUL ANGONE
The Christian
1-800-Heaven
"It's never too late to call"

Could This Be the Break?

But then, through a friend's sister's family friend, I got my big break. I had a phone interview with an executive producer at

NBC Sports. Take that, stupid "won't call me back" telemarketing company! The interview was for an unpaid internship, but hey, it was *NBC Sports*. I'd pay them to let me work there.

I dialed the number with nervous excitement. This was it; I knew it. Each ring an exciting yes to my years of no.

The interview went amazingly well. For about the first fifteen seconds. During the initial "hello" pleasantries.

After that it went straight down in wild, ravenous flames.

At one point in our brief conversation, the interviewer even went so far as to say, "Paul, these girls who connected you to me are like my daughters, and there's nothing in the world I wouldn't do for them. Except give someone with your little of experience this internship."

Wow. That stung a little. I couldn't even work for someone *for free*.

After that one, I had to take a long hike and sit next to a mountain stream. I prayed and cried a little while mosquitoes dined on my blood. This Great Recession was turning unbelievably depressing.

But I Want It Now!

I fully realize what a proud member I am of the get-it-now generation. The streaming, insta-everything, "if a website takes longer than three seconds to load, *I'm outta here*" generation. The time, effort, and art of making a mix tape are over. I thought success in my twenties would be the same way — instant, downloadable, and fully customizable at the touch of my screen.

I felt entitled to so much success and expected so little time and struggle to get there.

Yet, like that long road trip where you're nearing home and

really need to pee, everything takes a lot longer and is a tad more intense than you realized you could handle.

I was still looking for that one place with a welcome sign — that place where I could hang up my coat because I'd made it home. But my life was still a perpetual revolving door. Every building I entered turned me around and spit me right back out on the street.

Since I was about to get married, this revolving door was less than comforting.

"I Do"

I remember going to weddings and thinking to myself, *Wow, there's two people who really have life figured out*. Then you're the one getting married, and you realize you stand up there without a freaking clue.

Naomi's and my wedding day was beautiful and amazing, giving our lives to each other in front of our entire world while looking out over the Pacific Ocean. Naomi had seen me at my worst and still wanted to share a bed with me. Honestly, I'm still more shocked about it than you are.

Even as I was granted permission to "now kiss the bride," I glanced out of the corner of my eyes, expecting cameras and Ryan Seacrest to pop out and yell, "Gotcha! You've been part of a reality show called *A Girl Like This, Marry a Guy Like That? I DO* think this will be hilarious."

Hours later, I'd find myself on the dance floor with my wife and best friends, all of us with healthy amounts of Costco beer and bottles of Two-Buck Chuck (nicknamed for the delicious two-dollar bottles of wine from Trader Joe's that we splurged on) making everyone pump their legs so hard you'd think we were trying to stomp on the worm creatures from *Tremors*.

Our wedding was what you dream of.

Our honeymoon in Cabo, just as magical.

Sure, we hit some snags. Like on the second day of our honeymoon, when the pirate ship-led snorkeling excursion I had surprised Naomi with was boarded by really large men carrying really *real*, large guns.

"It's just the Coast Guard," the captain said, laughing at our worried faces. "We're just overcapacity with people. And a boat went under a few weeks back, so they're just being cautious."

"Umm … so will they make us turn back?" Naomi asked.

"Ha! No, my friend. We will fix this the Mexican way!"

This response was met with a round of applause and cheers from our fellow snorklers. Did I mention the pirate ship was also "all you can drink"?

And sure, thirty minutes later, Naomi got so seasick she was throwing up pieces of the wedding cake and cake from her seventh birthday, in between what I would describe as ferocious tears.

And sure, when we got to our "snorkeling" destination of slightly murky water that looked like a New York harbor after a flood, they kind of threw Naomi in the water to "help her" with her seasickness, which made her panic ever so slightly as she grabbed my shoulders like a cat trying to escape a pack of wolves, pushing me under the magnificent gray water that people were now clamoring to escape as millions of sea lice feasted on our skin.

The good news: I kept us afloat!

The bad news: I lost my wedding ring in the process!

But this was our honeymoon. We would not be fazed.

Okay, so sure, a few days later, a police officer threatened to arrest me for driving the "wrong way" on a "one-way street" — a street on which other cars were driving forward, backward, and sideways. Mexican jail felt like a honeymoon damper, so I reached into my pocket and held out a $20, and the kind officer gave me my license back.

Really, the police officer did us a favor. Now we had a shared story of marriage misadventure. We were growing closer by the Mexican minute.

Yet after the wedding and the honeymoon, you realize pretty quickly that the one amazing, magical day on which the world is rooting for you doesn't have the power to change all the days before and after, when the world keeps picking you last for kickball. Or worse yet, picking you as the kickball.

The Day After

I still didn't have a real, paying, "I can actually go to the hospital now for that thing" job. I was the guy in the "Made for TV" movie the mother pleads with her daughter not to marry. Without the cool hair or the motorcycle.

Really, how I passed the test and became a "husband," I haven't a clue. I'm looking at my qualifications and beginning to realize they are a little light.

I can't change the oil in a car by myself.

I have to concentrate really hard and close my eyes when someone says, "Grab me the socket wrench." The only thing I can build is a stack of dirty dishes and one out of five IKEA furnishings.

I have a very real fear that the fire alarm will start making those shrieking, "I'm dying" noises in the middle of the night and I won't be able to figure out how to turn it off before the landlord is summoned and has to do it for me. While he gives me a lecture about proper fire alarm testing. And makes me take notes.

I don't have a paying job. My dream of being an author is still in the "edits of the edits, redraft of the next draft" phase.

I thought when I got married I'd have my stuff together and know exactly what it means to be a husband. And even if I didn't, at least have a sufficient paycheck to buy my wife stuff when she realized this idiot doesn't have a clue.

This wasn't to be the case.

I spent four years in college learning how to be partially witty and mostly unemployed. And then I spent four afternoons with a married couple, for an hour and a half, learning how to be a husband. Something seems off.

Best Years of Your Life

Yet, even with failures and newfound insecurities piling up like wood at a winter cabin ready to be thrown into the fire, in no way do I wish I could go back.

I'm not trying to relive "the best years of my life," because right now with Naomi is pretty dang amazing. Even as I am engulfed again by the "what now?" vortex.

God was being faithful, even if I didn't fully understand the plan or the path. Naomi was being faithful, even if *she* didn't fully understand the plan or the path. We were in this together now, the three of us.

I'm realizing life is not about trying to recapture some idyllic memory of "home" that never really existed in the first place.

Life is not about making it back home; life is about making home right where you're at, with the tribe of people God gave you.

Each season carries with it the good, the bad, and the mediocre. If we see the good in every season only after the season is over, then we will never actually see any good. It's taken me way too long to realize that it's impossible to step into the future if you're obsessed with the past. And it's dangerous to step anywhere without a friend or two to back you up. Rob. Micah. Stanley. Naomi. *God.* I'm not strong enough or smart enough, and I don't own a fast enough horse, to try to do life as a Lone Ranger.

Mountaintop

We're still climbing mountains. We're sweating, stumbling, and dangerously low on oxygen.

But I have faith we're going to arrive at the top. Really, I do.

But it's going to take more time, stumbles, and failed plans than we ever could've planned. We're going to have to trust a few close friends and guides to hold the rope tight and not let us fall to our deaths. There will be times when everything will go wrong, and then your dog will die. You're probably going to ugly-cry in front of a few people, and it won't be pretty. You'll yell at someone you love, and love someone you shouldn't. There will be nights you'll want to scrap the whole climb, call your parents to pick you up in a helicopter, and live in their basement until you're sixty-five.

But we'll make it to the top. I know we will.

And when we finally stick our flag in the ground, victorious at last, we'll look around and feel the breeze, and it will be amazing! *For seven minutes.* Until someone says, "I really, *really* got to poo. Can we head back down now?"

So as we climb, let's not forget to pause, have a drink, and look at the amazing views along the way. Let's light a couple of fires and tell some stories. Let's share resources and lean into each other.

And do you know what would make this climb easier? Cutting off some deadweight. No, not each other, but past failures, guilt, bitterness, and regret. The climb is steep enough without trying to carry a dead yak from the past.

Life at the top is frickin' freezing with little air. You can't live at the top of the mountain. Our favorite memories will be the killer climb where we swore we were going to die next to our friends but somehow made it through. We'll tell *those* stories to our kids, not just the story of the view.

Let's thank God for the majesty of each step, not just when we deem life majestic.

We're still climbing and will be for a while. We're in this together. And I promise I'll shower more from here on out.

Hey, and while we're talking, do you want to lead for a little while? I'm sure you must be tired of staring at my backside, as highly toned with mush as it is. *You don't know where we're going?* Heck, I don't either. I kind of thought you would have noticed by now. *Do you need more oxygen?*

Anyhoo, let's just keep going. I'm sure we'll weave left and detour a little right. But really, there's no wrong way to walk forward.

Except if it's off a cliff. That would just be silly. But even then, a ledge of grace is waiting there to break our fall.

CHAPTER SIXTEEN

ALL
GROAN
UP

As we've slogged through the Great Recession of the twenty-first century, hasn't it felt like there's been an alien spacecraft hovering over us? The economy, layoffs, foreclosures, hiring freezes, wars, scandals, et cetera, et cetera — all seem to be little spacecrafts sent from the gigantic, looming mother ship of terror we can't see but whose shadow we sure can feel.

After years of writing and rewriting and rewriting my rewrites, I finally had the privilege of seeing a complete manuscript sent to publishers. Right as the first alien attack hit our city. Publishers were boarding up their windows, hiding under their big oak desks, and clutching their latest bestseller while I banged on the door, begging for someone to let me in. A couple of buildings downtown just exploded, and I was on the front step screaming my synopsis. Not an ideal combination.

Yet I was still sure a publisher would say yes. I had been working at it for five years now. Assuredly that was for a reason. As the manuscript went out, I began planning my speaking tour, working on my second book, and crafting my humorous, yet authentic answers for my "Serious Jibber-Jabber" with Conan O'Brien. I was ready.

All the while, Naomi and I were doing married life together, living in a small one-bedroom in a jam-packed, "intriguing" neighborhood in Glendale, California. There was rarely a dull moment.

One night, our entire street was swarming with undercover

cops who busted some neighbors making drugs two apartments down.

Another night we saw a bright flash outside our front window and stepped outside to see a beautiful white Mercedes engulfed in flames. As Naomi and I stood in our front yard with neighbors pouring out of their apartments to watch fifteen-foot hot orange streaks illuminate the sky, I remember thinking, *Wow, someone must have doused this car in gasoline. And Wow, more people live on this street than all of Connecticut. If Connecticut was 99 percent Armenian.*

Married life was an adventure. In every way. Naomi was in year two of working as a financial adviser as the entire financial industry began falling apart. Compared to the war Naomi entered into every day, the intensity of our neighborhood looked like a kindergarten class.

She was putting on the suit, and I was making the sandwiches. I brought in money here and there from odd jobs and writing assignments, yet she was clearly our financial rock in more ways than one.

Then it happened. After so many years of waiting and wondering, the manuscript went out to publishers, and the first round of responses trickled in from publishers. And each response was a polite "thanks but no thanks."

I was crushed. I felt like a failure, and, more painfully, I felt like I was failing Naomi. Her "big risk, big reward" investment in marrying me wasn't paying off.

Yet she never, ever made me feel like she was ready to "sell." She saw value in me that I couldn't see for myself, and she constantly reminded me of that fact when it felt to me like nothing but fiction.

Straight Talk from my Parents

Some days I would call my parents, wondering when I was going to get some straight talk from my dad about being "a man" — just forget this whole writing thing and get a steady, secure job.

Yet my parents were going through a massive transition of their own. They had left the church they started when I was a kid to pursue a career in business because they believed God was calling them into a new world.

The Great Recession wasn't making their transition easy either. My parents were going through their own season of learning how to be secure amid complete insecurity. All the words my dad had spoken from the pulpit about trusting God, even when everything is stripped away, was becoming all too real of a reality. Apparently stepping into the unknown to chase a dream and a calling wasn't just reserved for my generation.

So the only straight talk I received from my parents came in the form of words of encouragement, of faith and hope. Their belief in me was not a wave pulling in and out; it was a rock. And I in turn believed in them in the same way. We were supporting each other as we clung to a felt promise and purpose, even if none of us could actually see it any longer in the front store window.

But ...

My manuscript would go out to countless publishers over the course of a year, and every day, I'd wake up wondering if today was going to be the day when everything changed. I sat back, anxiously refreshing my email for that one yes that would change everything. Day after day. I waited and wondered if somehow my email was broken.

But ... that yes kept evading me.

I say *"but ..."* because that became the transition word I began to dread the most. Numerous publishers told me they liked the book, my voice, the story — with one publisher going so far as to write, "We think this book could be a bestseller, *BUT* ... we can't take a risk on an unknown author in this economic climate. Come back when you have a platform."

You know you're truly pursuing a dream when you feel like your heart has been broken into pieces and sold on the black market. Time and time again.

Cue the long walk on a pier in the fog, to violin music.

Or more accurately, cue a long hike above the Hollywood sign. Time and time again.

Hollywood Hills

I would climb these hills when I had no idea where else to go. I knew every bend. Every turn. Each "no" was following behind me, and I was trying my best to lose them.

Who knew on this day that what awaited me at the top would stay with me forever.

Over the last few months, I'd been climbing up the hill behind the famous Hollywood sign, feeling for the first time I was part of the Hollywood insider scene because I was seeing a side of it few others did.

And the view at the top was well, kind of ugly. I'd look over a brown, dying, dusty August landscape that made the California drought come to life. Then a little further beyond, I could make out some of LA, insulated in smog.

This wasn't exactly the Rocky Mountain hiking I grew up with. But if you're in LA and not sitting in the parking lot that some call the highway, you're grateful.

At the top of the Hollywood hills, for months I'd repeat the same prayer: *The desert is blossoming; the river is flowing; life abounds.*

I was warring for hope. Declaring life over my dry bones. But my heart and the landscape around me felt one and the same.

I was barely holding on for the weather to change.

Until this day.

I flew to the top of the trail and began my daily cleanse, washing away the rejection and failure that were suffocating me.

As I said the same words over and over, I looked down five feet in front of me in amazement.

The scorched earth all around was still dying and desolate, yet right in front of me was now a beautiful green patch filled with purple and yellow wildflowers.

It was like my words that had passed over countless times before brought life to the earth below.

I stood marveling at the beautiful flowers when two hummingbirds came dancing in and out, taking long drinks from this tiny oasis.

And as I saw the two hummingbirds, a truth filled me. It was as if God was speaking directly into my heart with a straw: *Paul, your desert will blossom. And it's to bring life to those around you.*

It was another portal of encouragement. An unexpected gift of vision and clarity that cut through the crap and went straight to my core. When everything was feeling purposeless, God was reminding me of the whole purpose.

In reality, the writing on the wall was smacking me in the face, brick by brick. Yet I felt like everyone and everything important to me were shouting, "Just hold on!"

It was time to either quit this dream or find another way.

I decided to do both.

Becoming All Groan Up

I called my literary agents, thanked them, and told them I wanted to end my contract. It was time to start all over. Again. I didn't have a plan. Yet I knew this was the first step to finding one.

Then Naomi told me she thought I should get a master's degree. *Great idea*, I thought. *Not only will I not be bringing in much money, but I'm going to start taking more of what we have.* I politely declined.

Yet Naomi did not let up. She felt so strongly I should pursue a master's degree that it became a question not of "what if" but of "which one."

I chose to pursue a master's in organizational leadership at Azusa Pacific University and oftentimes felt out of place in a roomful of working professionals. Yet by the third class session, a classmate mentioned the school was looking to hire someone in the graduate admissions office, and pretty soon I found myself hired for the position and back in the cubicle.

Now I was receiving a steep discount for my master's degree and learning a ton, and I was getting paid in the process. Naomi's leap of faith and her belief in my future that propelled me to go after a master's degree when I didn't have a job or a clue were paying off.

Yes, I was back in a job that was nowhere near my dream. But I was gathering more sticks and supplies, which I hoped one day to light on fire. To give others warmth, not burn down my own house. I was strategically settling for a season to work on a new route toward the dream I felt I was not supposed to let go of.

Times Keep On Changing

There was still never a dull moment in our neighborhood. The newest development was a thirtysomething gentleman in tall white socks, basketball shorts, and a collared shirt (to class himself up), who stood on a corner next to us, day and night, selling something other than Cutco knives, as far as I could tell. He was a people watcher, that little rascal, and he especially enjoyed watching Naomi day in and day out as she went to work and came home. He seemed especially concerned with the brand of her dress pants because he was always staring at the back of them when she walked away. He must've had sisters and was looking for Christmas ideas. But when he left a note on Naomi's car that read, "Give me a call sometime, and we'll grab drinks," I felt like it was time for us to move on.

Plus, the one-bedroom was going to be a little tight. Since Naomi was pregnant! With my baby, not the drug dealer's. Just in case there was any doubt on your end.

With a baby coming, I signed up for extra classes for my master's degree to try to finish before the due date. The only pages I was writing now were for research papers, my dreams of writing a book simmering on low. But as my master's program neared the end, I convinced my professor to allow me to create a website for my final project that was based on research I had done to help twentysomethings struggling with "what now?"

On a day in December, I presented my website, AllGroanUp .com, to a roomful of family, friends, professors, classmates, and coworkers. And a few weeks later, they still let me graduate.

Naomi and I geared up to launch AllGroanUp.com into the World Wide Web as she, more importantly, geared up to launch a little human into the world. As we went to hospital classes to learn how to breathe (for her) and not pass out (for me), I looked around at the men holding pillows and perplexed looks and thought, *Let the next season of cluelessness begin!*

At nine months pregnant, Naomi was still up on her feet, helping me print and cut out promo cards to mail out for the launch of All Groan Up. Then later that same night, we were rushing to the hospital for the biggest launch of our life.

The hospital classes didn't teach me what to do when you feel like you're going to pass out *and* throw up at the exact same time. After a night of pushing and breathing, our baby was right there but would not come out. A small army of nurses and doctors sped into the room as I heard "umbilical cord wrapped around the neck." I shot a prayer to God with a rocket launcher and watched with suspended helplessness. My heart that stopped beating for five minutes exploded with emotion as I saw our healthy little girl make an entrance at her birthday party in grand style.

The Blur of Birth

The next few weeks and months were a blur as I finally realized why sleep deprivation is such an effective torture technique. So, of course, why not launch a website at the same time? With "plentiful" amounts of free time, sleep, and sanity, I wrote with ease.

For years I'd been pleading with agents and publishers that twentysomethings were going through a long, intense transition process, and someone needed to help them through the muck. Now it was time for me to just go do it. I stopped waiting for a publisher's permission to tell my story and just began sharing it.

I learned that waiting for the right time to pursue one's dreams is like waiting for enough sleep to be a good parent.

Over another year of grinding, unglamorous, sweaty work, I wrote to a small, growing, passionate twentysomething tribe, while Naomi edited in her "free" time. I began connecting with my readers — emerging adults who felt their twenties were caked in massive amounts of *un-success*, just like I had felt.

My own professional failures were letting me speak into the metanarrative of my generation. All the dark and dismal places of defeat that I'd frequently visited were helping show people a way out of theirs.

At my job, I transferred from the admissions office to marketing, and for the first time in my life, I felt like I truly fit well at a job. Yet at 5:00 a.m., on lunch breaks, late into the night, I was still writing. It had become something I could not NOT do.

Yet I'd been writing about this "twentysomething story" for eight years now. AllGroanUp.com was growing, but it wasn't a smashing success. It was taking up a lot of time and bringing in zero money. A question began to plague me like ants crawling on a chocolate bar: *Is this dream worth it?*

There's always the ugly side of chasing a dream. Relationships, status, sanity, safety — name the cost, and it's been paid before. Status quo can't coexist with a dream. Like putting a lion in your living room and asking it to play nice. The old way of doing things, one way or another, ceases to exist. Was the cost worth it? What's perseverance, and what's plain stupidity? How far is far enough when it doesn't seem to be getting you anywhere?

I remember one afternoon when Naomi, who had been supporting this dream longer than any sane person should, just looked at me and said, "Is it time to let this go?"

I didn't have an answer. But I knew she was right. I'm stubborn, but I don't want to live my entire life as a complete ass. Eight years is long enough. I knew I was close to the end.

Then for the 1,365th time, I went to a coffee shop to write. I wrote a list called "21 Secrets for your 20s," a compilation of ideas and articles I'd been crafting during those eight years. I posted the list on my website without thinking much about it.

Four days later, so many people were reading it that the website crashed. Twice.

"21 Secrets for your 20s" has now been read by more people than live in Wyoming and Barbados combined. My tipping point finally tipped, leading to my debut book *101 Secrets for Your Twenties*. A completely different book than the one I had been writing all along, but it was the book I needed nine years to get to. And after those nine years, once it finally hit, I had a month to turn a blog article into a book while working a full-time job and reminding my family that I still existed. Some seasons you can't force to speed up and some seasons you can't stop from slowing down. It's kept rolling full-speed downhill ever since.

And ten years later, you and I are now holding the book that started it all.

The Crappy Truth to Chasing a Dream

Every no is leading you toward a bigger yes. Sounds like I'm being the butt-clown on stage with a fake tan now, but I promise it's true. (*And I can prove it to you for $199 …*)

As a writer, leader, entrepreneur, husband, wife, dreamer, you sometimes have to be willing to fail first.

The hero always experiences an "all is lost" moment before the dramatic rise. You can't create a masterpiece without mashing, sculpting, and molding the clay — and then throwing the whole thing in the fire.

World changers typically have their greatest impact where they have experienced the most personal pain.

For me this road has been anything but easy, and I still have a long way to go. But I needed to learn how to walk on in spite of failure and rejection if I was going to try to help people do the same. And be fine with looking like a darn fool on many occasions along the way.

I learned that those we partner with can make or break the whole ride. In business, in friendships, in love, in faith. If we partner with people out of desperation or fear, if we choose relationships from our insecurities, if we don't choose wisely the people who walk with us, it will make the journey a lot more perilous than it has to be. With all the stumbles and falls coming our way, we need some secure people to pick us up.

I've learned that most of the time we don't choose between chasing our dream and paying the bills. We do both at the same time. For years. The job feeding us while we work on our dream. And the dream feeding us while we work at our job.

I learned that if we're going to get up at 5:00 a.m. to work on our dream before we drive in at 8:00 a.m. to work at our work, we better love the process of our dream more than just the desired outcome.

And really the truth is that you don't chase a dream; you grow one. It's just like a farmer whose whole existence relies on one simple belief: If we plant something in good soil and consistently water it, God will spark life underground.

Now I get to write and speak full-time. Then as Naomi goes back to work part-time, we trade off watching our two girls during the day. (Yay to another birth of another amazing girl!

Yay to two girls under two years old! Yay to no sleep and sanity!)
It's busy. It's amazing. It's my dream in real life.

Yet I still struggle. I'm living the dream I've been working
toward for the last decade, and yet sometimes the anxiety and
pressure make me want to curl up with Netflix and just keep
streaming.

I compare myself to more talented, successful authors. I let
mean things written about me on the Internet actually mean
something to me. I all too quickly lose vision, motivation, and
inspiration.

I have to keep reminding myself that motivation and creativity are rarely things that just happen. The inspiration we need to
find our dreams and grow our dreams is not something mythi-
cal; it's methodic.

Sometimes the most inspired thing you can do is to just keep
showing up when inspiration is out on a Caribbean cruise and
not returning any of your phone calls. You can only find inspiration by continuing to move forward when you're completely
uninspired. *The act of doing* can often be the only thing that can
dislodge the motivation that has been stuck.

You don't wait for inspiration; you fight for it.

So if you don't know what your dream is, do something. Try
something. Take a chance. As you pursue something, the main
thing you thought you were pursuing may slowly fade away as
the actual main thing begins to reveal itself.

I thought I was supposed to be a writer. But when I finally
reached the top of that path, I was met with a big barbed wire
fence with a sign that read, "Road Closed. Trespassers Will Be
Shot!"

I cried. I gave up. Pursuing a dream felt like a long, ungodly
trek fit for a 1970s low-budget sci-fi movie.

Then slowly I began exploring other creative ways to reach the same destination. I learned, with much fear and hesitation, to develop skills as a blogger, marketer, speaker, entrepreneur, editor of both videos and print materials, graphic designer, photographer, communicator, and collaborator with others I meet along the way. And then, best of all, I learned how to be a better writer! I learned that part of my "Road Closed" wasn't just the external conditions but the fact that my skill level wasn't strong enough to climb over the obstacles.

I don't write this to say, "Look how talented I am!" because I'm not. I write it to encourage all of us that the detours we'll come across along the way aren't distractions from our dreams; they are possibly the strategic paths that lead straight to the heart of them. You need to stand on top of your "Road Closed" if you're going to help others do the same.

So if you think you know what your dream is but you're afraid it may never see the light of day, if your inspiration is running on empty, maybe your purpose is so important that it can only be forged in the difficult and the dire. Maybe your dream needs to sit in the desert for a while so you can learn how to make it survive.

No water, no food, and no shade — it's easy to die in the desert, no doubt about it. But if we can stay alive here, with all our old comforts burned and blown away, well, then we can stay alive, and thrive, anywhere else.

I had to learn to sit and be still. I had to truly believe God for who he is and not for what I perceived he was or was not doing.

I was constantly striving to *be someone* without realizing Someone else was in control all along. And to truly be someone, I needed to learn how to truly be myself.

We are, each of us, tailor-made. I don't say this to increase the narcissistic knock on our generation. I say this to praise the Master Chef and the intricate, artistic, and exquisite ingredients he's created you with. You have what I would call your own "signature sauce." Your values, strengths, challenges, vision, talents, experiences, and failures. The injustices that break your heart. The music that makes you dance. The unique mix of people in your life. Your past, present, and future story. And even the heat being applied to you! All of these ingredients, and much more, create in you a signature sauce that gives the world a substance and flavor no one else can provide.

Yet understanding the "soul of your sauce" doesn't happen in an afternoon; it's an ongoing discovery. It's understood in solitude. Honest reflection. Failed experiments that singe your eyebrows. Through the guidance and wisdom of others. By the leading of God's craftsman, artisan, and creator Spirit calling it out in each of us. And we might hear this voice more clearly and crisply in the painful, vulnerable moments when we feel like we can't even boil water than when we're winning a trophy for the best sauce this side of the Mississippi.

The pain you are experiencing now may be your life's purpose later.

And if not, it will at least make a good story! People love hearing about other people's crap. If that wasn't the case, why else would there be reality TV?

The Truth to "Making It"

In college, for the most part, we learned how to regurgitate truth, not own it. We rented the answers until semester's end, and then we pawned them off for $10.50 at our school's bookstore. We played the game for good grades without realizing the real tests were nowhere near the classroom.

Yet becoming an adult is not a onetime thing. You grow into growing up, each season bringing with it things you're going to have to secretly Google to figure out how to do.

I know we have this yearning to "arrive." To make it. We want to unpack our bags. Paint the house the color we want. Tear down a few needless walls and build a huge custom desk that will never leave the room.

However, every time we think we've made it, we look out the window to see a U-Haul truck waiting to take us to the next town.

But maybe not making it is a gift. If you've arrived, why bother still exploring?

When you've made it, why put in the extra time? Why battle the hard questions? Why push yourself?

There is no need to create anything more when you think you've made all you can make. Maybe every person who "made it" was simply stopping short.

Maybe those of us who feel very "unmade" were simply meant to create more.

Everything in Its Season

In American culture specifically, I think we operate on this idea that life is a linear, stair-step progression. And to succeed we need to keep climbing faster and farther (and push others out of the way) until we reach the top.

But I'm realizing more and more that life is not a linear progression for us to command and conquer. We don't ever just fully "arrive."

No, life is lived in overlapping seasons and cycles for us to recognize and act accordingly — each season completely necessary to produce the next; the death and decay of one piece of fruit falling to the ground, leading to the growth and rebirth of another.

Truly successful people aren't conquering these seasons; they're living wisely within them.

Same Life, Different Seasons

And just like our world experiences different seasons at different places, you may be experiencing different seasons in different parts of your life.

It may feel like winter in your career, but spring in your relationships. Maybe your faith feels like it's in autumn as you've been stripped of all the leaves you covered yourself with, while your dreams experience a hot and dusty summer.

Or maybe it's just a flat-out cold, harsh winter everywhere in your life, and you're hunkered next to a stove with this book, trying to warm your frigid bones. Man, I've been there. Winter will end. I promise.

(Re)Born Again

I'm beginning to picture myself as one of those intricately designed clocks with inner gears that run at various speeds, are different sizes, and even go in opposite directions. They may not be moving at the speed and the direction I want them to go, and yet these overlapping circles, all working together, are somehow moving time forward.

Instead of dreading the cycle we're in, we really should be

thankful for it. We should own whichever season we're in. We should sink deep into it and ask ourselves what we should be doing in this season. Is it time to plant or to uproot? Is it time to settle or to explore? Time to rest or to run full tilt? Time to work in a cubicle or to light it on fire?

We're not born once. We're born again and again, and again and again and again. The new sights and sounds, frightening as they are exhilarating, every single time. But in every birth and in every death, God is in fact moving us toward the life he promised; the details just won't look anything like we expected.

As I move further into groan-up life and experience seasons where it feels like I'm stringing together one ugly day after another, I'll hope in God that something breathtaking is still happening.

I'll trust God to infect me with peace when the surrounding world feels plagued with everything contrary to it.

I'm sure there'll be questions and struggles, times when I will feel alone and lost. I'm sure I'll stumble and fall, adding a couple more scars next to all of the rest of them.

But as I sit here on the brink of the new unknowns, I thank him.

Thank you, God, for all the ways you've been faithful, even when I wasn't. Thank you for snatching me from midair, providing your ledges of grace. Thank you for loving me as your child. As if I deserved it.

Thank you, heavenly Father, for letting me be born, that I might actually live.

THANK YOU,
AND AN OFFER FOR YOU

Thank you for reading this book and officially joining this "Groan Up" community. (I signed you up upon purchase and will be automatically charging your credit card $19.23 (plus an additional $75 startup fee), unless you call this number 1-737-ZI07-0000 three days ago.

I hope you read this book in community and have found the conversations more insightful than the words on these pages. And I'd love to join you in this conversation. Join the community at AllGroanUp.com to find overwhelming amounts of truth, hope, and hilarity as we tell the story of our generation, and for our generation. Then if you want to talk more with me specifically, email me at paul@allgroanup.com.

Also I am passionate about helping others discover their own unique "signature sauce." If you'd like more intentional, strategic guidance from me, check out the amazing program and community we've created at SignatureSauce.com. Let's figure out the "soul of your sauce" and then construct an action plan to create a purpose-filled, massively meaningful life based on your unique mix of ingredients. Put AllGroanUp in the promo code, and I'll make sure to hook you up with a nice discount! Let's not have this conversation begin and end with this book.

All right, I think I've accomplished everything I wanted to in this afterword. Let's see:

- ☑ Wrap up all the things.
- ☑ Say good-bye to beautiful reader, you. And if I may say so myself, you look amazing today. Seriously, did you do something different with your hair?
- ☑ Compliment amazing reader, you, so you'll hopefully write nice things about this book on the Internet. I read reviews. My wife reads them. My daughters read them. My daughters cry when the reviewers say mean things. With their cute little eyes and belief in their daddy . . .
- ☑ Guilt-trip reader.
- ☑ Drag out word count for bigger payout.

Done and done!

Again, thank you.

Really, there's not much else to do other than . . .

ACKNOWLEDGMENTS

First and foremost, thank you to my wife and best friend, Naomi Angone. Thank you for editing this book more times than I can count, over more years than I want to remember. You have the patience and the grace of a saint!

Thank you to my amazing daughters, Hannalise and Sierrah. As I watch you both create, dream, and dance, it daily encourages and reminds me to do the same. You both are dripping with the Master Chef's intentionality and purpose.

Thank you, Kevin Thomas and Sandy Hermansen, for possessing massive amounts of mercy when reading those first four rambling, rough chapters and somehow still encouraging me to keep writing.

Thank you, Cody Gore, Matt Spahn, Ben Patterson, Mike Yankoski, Becky Peterson, Jeff Hunt, and Emily Hughes, for reading subsequent versions of this book and giving me input and encouragement to keep going. And when I felt like slamming my computer on the floor and jumping on it repeatedly, like a seven-year-old throwing a tantrum at Toys "R" Us, I'd often reread your words, set my computer down, and walk away slowly. My computer thanks you as well.

Thank you, my brain trust — Brent Boekestein and Jonathan Miller — for invaluable advice and support during some difficult times.

Thank you, Wayne Jacobsen, for letting a complete stranger take you out to lunch, pick your brain, invite you to read the book, and receive from you incredible insight. The book would look very different if you hadn't gotten involved.

Thank you, Sam Melvin, for being the most fun and encouraging person to talk through ideas with.

Thank you, Rob, Micah, Stanley, and the countless other friends who did life with me along this journey and taught me so much along the way.

Thanks, Goleta Coffee in Goleta, California, for being a funky place to be creative. Many of these early pages were penned there. Thank you, Starbucks, for never kicking me out and for free refills.

Thank you, Ray Rood, for all the morning coffees, encouraging me to step out on my own and into my future.

I listened to much of the same music over and over while writing this book: Johnny Cash, Passion Pit, Ryan Adams, Paul Simon, Bon Iver, Arcade Fire, Postal Service, Guster, and M83. Yet nothing compared to how much I listened to Sufjan Stevens. Sufjan, I have to specifically thank you. For a year, during the hardest and bleakest time of writing, your music was the only thing that kept me going. Every one of your songs was like you were personally giving me permission to be creative and push through. Thank you for your inspiration, honesty, and ingenuity, and for making music that encouraged my faith.

Finally, a HUGE thank you to all the talented professionals at HarperCollins and Zondervan who helped bring this book to life. Tom Dean for believing in me and this project from the beginning. Then my wonderful editors, Sandy Vander Zicht and Dirk Buursma, for all the incredible ways you "whispered" into this book. Your editing was masterful.

101 Secrets for Your Twenties

Paul Angone

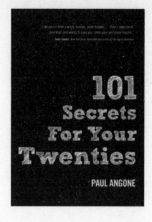

Every twentysomething needs a little black book of secrets. Our twenties are filled with confusion, terrible jobs, anticipation, disappointment, cubicles, breakups, transition, quarter-life crises, loneliness, post-college what-the-heck, moderate success sandwiched in between complete failure, and we need a worn, weathered guide stashed somewhere close by to help shed some light on this defining decade.

This is that book.

Expanded from the blog post "21 Secrets for Your 20s" that spread like Internet wildfire, 101 Secrets for Your Twenties will encourage, inspire, prompt a plethora of LOLs, and kick-start your life forward with its witty, honest, and hilarious wisdom-stuffed pearls to help you rock life in your twenties.

Published by
Moody Publishers, Chicago, Illinois, 2013